The House of Christian Contrasts

James A. Fowler

C.I.Y. Publishing
P.O. Box 1822
Fallbrook, CA 92088-1822

THE HOUSE OF CHRISTIAN CONTRASTS

© 2018 by James A. Fowler

All rights reserved.
No part of this publication may be reproduced without the prior written permission of the author, except for excerpts in book reviews and quotations that are accurately cited.

Published by
C.I.Y. Publishing
P.O. Box 1822
Fallbrook, CA 92088-1822
www.christinyou.net

ISBN – 978-1-929541-34-8

Scripture quotations are from the New American Standard Bible. Copyright © 1960, 1962, 1963, 1968, 1971, 1972, 1973, 1975 by the Lockman Foundation, LaHabra, California.

Printed in the United States of America

TABLE OF CONTENTS

Introduction 1

Focusing on the Foundation 17

Examining the Framework 43

Experiencing the Finishing Work 73

    The Experiences of Life 86
    Affectivity 103
    The Seen Perspective 105
    The Unseen Perspective 120
    Eternal Weight of Glory 134

Seen / Unseen Diagrams 148

Conclusion 175

FOREWORD

The thesis of this book was first developed for a conference in Dalton, Pennsylvania, sponsored by Don Frantz and the Binghamton, New York Bible Study Group, in May 2008. That preliminary form of the study was put on the backburner, and was only developed more fully in the form presented in this text when preparing for a conference sponsored by Don Burzynski at the Cross-life Counselling Center in Vero Beach, Florida in 2015.

This is a rather unorthodox theological study, constructed with the analogy of a physical house, with the designed intent to provide a comprehensive outline and analysis of the Christian gospel. This study fits within the category of philosophical theology, as distinct from historical theology, dogmatic theology, biblical theology, or systematic theology. Although there is an abundance of scriptural documentation, the basic structure of the study is formed by logical constructs of the major Christian premises, accompanied by explanatory transitions that hold the various parts of the thesis together.

The original spoken form of the teaching has been edited and reformatted, but we have retained much of the informal phraseology of the spoken words within the written form of presenting the thoughts in book form. In addition, we have taken the graphics that were displayed as PowerPoint slides in the teaching series, and utilized the diagrams and textual data as illustrations within the text of this book.

As an author who is always attempting to articulate the Christian gospel in a more meaningful way, I have found the formulation of the components of this study to be useful in providing a unifying structure to the Christian faith. I believe that readers who take the time to read and think through the concepts of this book may be able to put together some pieces of the gospel message that might have appeared dissonate or disparate. That does not imply that this study can provide an air-tight construct of human logic that explains Christian thought beyond all reasonable doubt, for God's action in His Son Jesus Christ will forever contain the element of divine mystery concerning the spiritual actions of the infinite God on behalf of mankind.

May the reader approach this text with an open mind, receptive to the "Spirit of truth," and desirous of better understanding what God has done and is doing.

                                      January 15, 2018
                                      James A. Fowler

The House of Christian Contrasts

Introduction

Although I have engaged in some home construction over the years, I do not consider myself an accomplished construction worker. While building an addition to our home, I poured concrete for the foundation, framed the walls and roof, ran all the electrical wiring for lights and switches, attached all the sheetrock, laid the flooring, and painted all the walls and trim. The only thing I did not attempt was the "mudding" of the sheetrock joints. Overall, it was an extended and exhausting endeavor.

Such engagement in physical building construction caused me to recognize the complexity of the task of building a house. Now, drawing upon such insights, I commence to consider the mental constructs of "The House of Christian Contrasts." In many ways, the complexity of explaining how the various parts of Christian thought build upon one another and fit together in a complete and orderly manner is as strenuous and exhausting as physical construction of a building.

Such philosophical and theological analysis is what I have been trained to do in my educational background, and therefore what I am better suited to engage in rather than in physical house construction. The natural inclination of my mental processes tends to gravitate toward attempting to bring the various parts of any topic together in an integrated, broad perspective. It is just the way that God seems to have wired my brain. I am always seeking to see the "big picture." Had I not been called by God to study philosophy and theology, I might have pursued being a "systems analyst" in the business world, attempting to facilitate the organizational flow and efficiency of a business model.

Prior to our looking at the various parts of "The House of Christian Contrasts," we will need to do what any contractor involved in home-construction must do – look at the blueprints to visualize where the project is going.

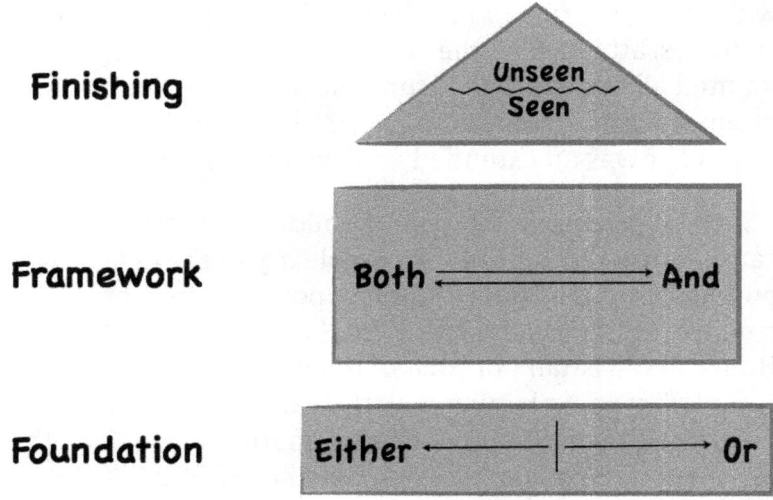

The first of our blueprint pages reveals the general outline that we will be following in this study. Every house must have a **foundation**, on which there will be constructed a **framework**, topped or capped with the **finishing** work.

In constructing our "House of Christian Contrasts," our **foundation** of thought will be the **Either/Ors** that underlie our thinking as Christians. There are basic antitheses that are presuppositional to the construction of Christian thought. These opposing personages and ideas form the fundamental foundations of our thinking. Good and evil, for example, are never merged in Christian thinking. Unlike the monistic idea that good and evil are fundamentally one – that there is some good in evil, and some evil in all good, symbolized by the *yin/yang* illustration – Christianity asserts that God alone is essentially Good and the source of all Good, and in Him there is no evil.

The **framework** of Christian thought is formulated in the **both/ands** of dialectic thought. This particular feature of "The House of Christian Contrasts" has been thoroughly considered in a previous book entitled *Two Sides of Every Coin: A Dialectic Formatting of Christian Thought,* which contains one hundred and thirty charts showing the balanced tension of Christian thought in a variety of categories. Though there is a tendency – we might say a temptation – among Christian thinkers to attempt to frame everything in either/ors, wherein one's particular doctrinal conclusions are the only correct formulations, and those who disagree with our conclusions are wrong and heretical, we must avoid framing all Christian thinking in contrasting either/ors which fail to recognize that there is an opposing side.

The **finishing** features of Christian thought take us beyond mere thought-categories, beyond mere ideology, and take us into the practical and experiential categories of living the Christian life day by day. We will attempt to explicate this practical "finishing work" of the Christian life, by differentiating between the **"seen"** and **"unseen"** perspectives of what is happening in our lives. Our natural tendency as human beings here on earth is to view situations viscerally and react to the "seen" exigencies of life from a temporal perspective. But as Christians, we should be more aware of spiritual and "unseen" realities, of God's working in our lives via the Spirit of Christ, of His dynamic grace provision that can be personally realized by our receptivity of faith. This latter theme of the experiential finishing-work in our Christian lives is intended to be the predominant focus of this study.

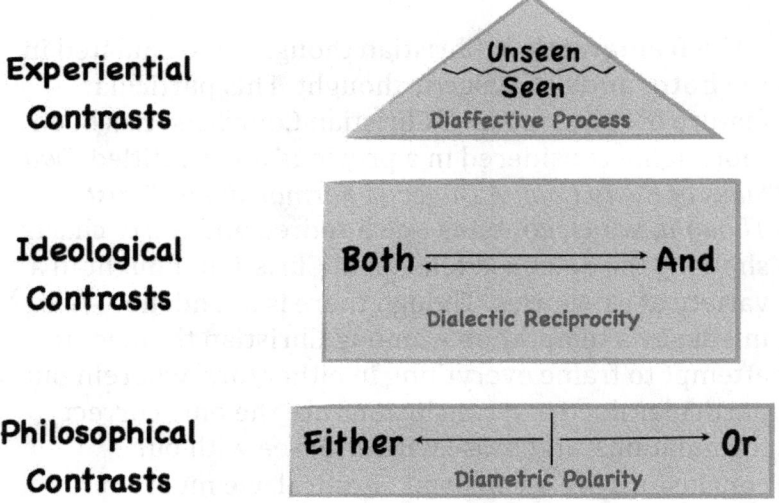

On the next page of the blueprints, we note that this **"House of Christian Contrasts"** has...

• **Philosophical and Theological contrasts** that are foundational.

• **Ideological Contrasts** wherein we form our doctrinal understanding, and

- **Experiential Contrasts** wherein we see how our Christian thinking must be translated into the behavioral action of our Christian lives, i.e. how we allow the life of Jesus Christ to be lived out in our behavior.

   The foundational philosophical and theological contrasts are constructed in the Either/Ors that form a **"Diametric Polarity"** of contrasted entities. Diametric comes from the same root word as "diameter," signifying the two most opposite points on the far sides of a circle. When we "measure through" the circle (the etymology of "diameter"), these are the extreme opposite points. The foundation of Christian thought is formed on the "diametric polarity" of opposite contrasting concepts. There is a "diametric polarity," for example, between God and Satan.

   The framework of Christian thought is best expressed in the ideological contrasts as they are formulated in the Both/Ands of constantly maintained **"Dialectic Reciprocity,"** wherein each theme or thesis is allowed to continuously "talk through" to the other concept. That is the etymological meaning of "dialectic," to "talk through" and relate to the other idea, without trying to force either tenet into priority over the other, but allowing them to interact with one another in a tensioned thinking that seems to be difficult for Western thinkers.

   The practical "finishing features" of the experiential contrasts of Christian living will be formulated in the tension of the "seen" and "unseen" perspectives, the contrasting points of views, or frames of reference by which we perceive what is going on in our lives. I have alliteratively labelled this part of the construction as the **"Diaffective Process."** Diaffective means that we move "through" the natural human "affects" of how we are personally affected by all that is happening around us. As Christians, we want to see what God is doing in our lives, and allow Him to be and do what He wants to be and do.

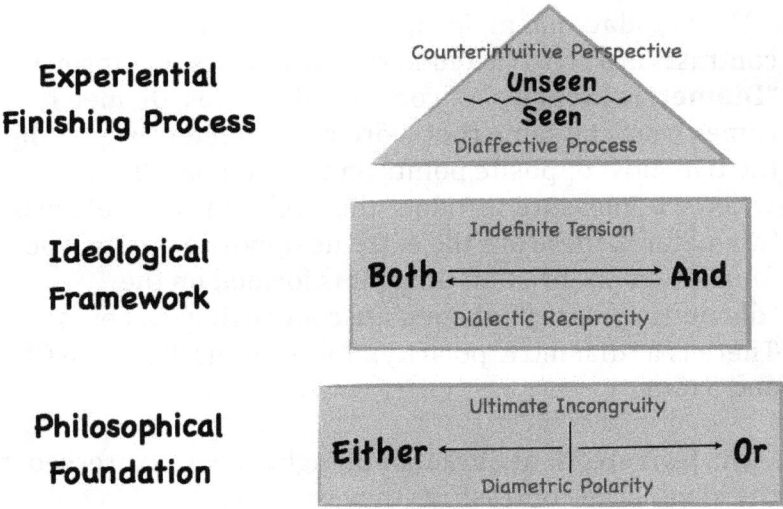

In the midst of discussing the Philosophical Foundation of our "Christian House of Contrasts," constructed with the Either/Ors of Diametric Polarity, we will note an **"Ultimate Incongruity."** The "Ultimate Incongruity" involves the difficulty of understanding and explaining how the Absolutely GOOD God who created the entire universe could, would, and did allow for evil to exist in the good world that He created. This dilemma has been a subject that the philosophers and theologians have struggled with for many centuries. We will have to address that problem!

The Ideological Framework of our Christian House is constructed of the Both/And contrasts of Dialectic Reciprocity. This dialectic reciprocity involves a problematic "**Indefinite Tension**" that many Western thinkers find difficult to maintain. We of the Western world, steeped as we are in Greek, specifically Aristotelian, categories of human thinking, find it very difficult to allow ideas to remain in limbo, without resolving them in some kind of perceived certainty. We want definite doctrinal propositions that we consider to be "absolute truths," set in concrete. The latitude and flexibility of dialectic reciprocity is hard to accept for Western thinkers.

The Experiential Finishing Process of our Christian thought construction will be formulated in the contrasts of the "seen" and the "unseen", in what we have labelled the "Diaffective Process." But, in "moving through" our natural human "affects" and subjective reactions, we do not want to project the idea that the Christian individual can arrive at an elevated spiritual experience that floats above the tough times of life here on earth. The "seen" and the "unseen" are always, until the day we die, a simultaneous experience. Despite whatever spiritual "unseen" perspective we might participate in, we are still human and will inevitably endure the trials of everyday life. We will bounce back and forth, kind of like a ping-pong ball, between the "seen" and "unseen" points of reference. That is the way it's going to be for human beings here on earth! The apostle Paul in his spiritual maturity could still say, "not that I have already arrived, or am already perfect" (Phil. 3:12).

In our attempt as Christians to see beyond the "seen" circumstances of our physical existence here on earth in order to see the "unseen" realities of God's spiritual working in our lives, this will necessitate the spiritual awareness of a "**Counterintuitive Perspective**" that

"God's ways are not our ways, and God's thoughts are not our thoughts" (Isa. 55:8,9). The divine perspective takes into account contingencies and provisions beyond what human wisdom can imagine or think (cf. Eph. 3:20).

Transitions in the various portions of this structure of contrasts

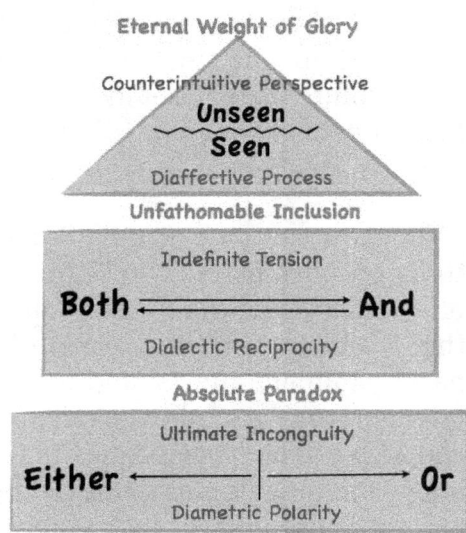

On the next sheet of our blueprints of "The Christian House of Contrasts" we will look at the "Transitions in the various portions of this structure of contrast."

The Foundation of the Either/Ors with its "Diametric Polarity" and problematic "Ultimate Incongruity" might be solidly poured, but then we must confront the issue of whether human thought can logically allow for an either/or to become a both/and. Human logic indicates that if we have a solid or rigid either/or, either this or that construct, then it is illogical to think that an either/or can become a both/and. At that transition point, then, we have to consider the distinctively Christian postulate of the Incarnation of Jesus Christ.

That reality is what Soren Kierkegaard called, "**The Absolute Paradox**."

The transition from the Dialectic Reciprocity of the Both/Ands with their "indefinite tension" requires another distinctively Christian transformation that allows the objective truths of Christian thought to allow for individual human beings to participate in what God has made available in His Son, Jesus Christ. Historically and theologically we affirm that Jesus lived the life that He lived, and died the death that He died, and rose from the dead to ascend into heaven, but, how are we brought into this narrative of God's dealing with mankind? Is this Christian thought-structure more than a belief-system that we assent to and affirm? How do we get involved in HIS story? That transition requires an **"Unfathomable Inclusion"** in the very life of the historical Jesus who has become the "experiential Jesus," the risen and living Spirit of Christ.

Only those who have participated in the "unfathomable inclusion" into the life of Jesus, and have received His very LIFE into their spirits, can make the transition into the "diaffective process" of the simultaneous experience of the "seen" and "unseen" of the Christian life with a "counterintuitive perspective" that is beyond human thought-categories. Only genuine, Christ-indwelt Christians enter into the experiential finishing process of Christian living. And in that process, they can experience the "Eternal Glory" of the presence of the Triune God and His activity. This "eternal glory" is not a reality that is delayed in some expected future event of residence in heaven, but is the glorious reality of bearing God's glorious character unto His own glory day by day, and moment by moment, in the "NOW" of our Christian experience.

We have looked at the blueprints of our Christian House, and now we will proceed to consider the various parts of the house, as they relate analogously or figuratively to the construction of a physical house.

You will soon discover that what we are calling "The House of Christian Contrasts" is rather different than the "Religious Structure" that many people are familiar with when they think of Christianity. It might be said that we are thinking far more abstractly than the religious form that prevails in general church circles. The "religious structure" is often built with the concrete of firmly asserted dogmatism and the absolutes of doctrinal certainty in a religious belief-system. It tends to take this form.

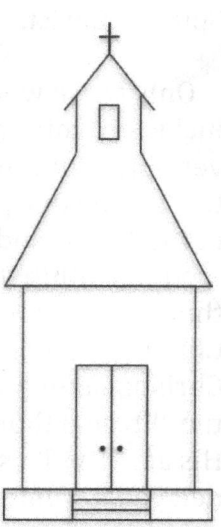

Religious Structure

Has a different form than the philosophical and theological form of the house of contrasts that we are constructing.

Built with the concrete of firmly asserted dogmatism and the absolutes of doctrinal certainty in a religious belief-system.

Now, it is not our objective to denigrate or deprecate the traditional church that so many are used to and familiar with, but our construction of Christian thought will stretch the horizons, and cause people to think through the premises of Christian reality.

It is always important to begin a construction project with a firm **FOUNDATION**, which is the load-bearing part of any structure, providing support for all of other parts.

The Foundation

The foundation is the load-bearing part of a structure that provides support for all other parts.

Any structure will only be as stable as the foundation on which it is built.

Jesus referred to the importance of how and where we construct the foundation of our house, when He used the analogy of building a house on the rock or on the sand (Matt. 7:24-27).

Foundations of physical structures

Are they built on rock or sand?

Foundations of physical structures

Not the most aesthetic part of the structure.

Often buried beneath the ground

Upon the foundation, the builder constructs the framework of the house. The framework is the skeleton that provides form and design to a building or structure. The framework of a physical house is comprised of floor joists, wall studs, and the framing of doors and windows.

The Framework

The framework is the skeleton that provides form and design to a building or structure.

The framework of a house is comprised of floor joists, wall studs, and the framing of doors and windows, etc.

Framing a house or structure

The floors and walls take form

The floor plan becomes evident

The framework of our figurative "House of Christian Contrasts" is structured in the balanced tensions of ideological contrasts. This allows the framework of Christian thought to have form with flexibility.

The Framework of Christian Thought

can be structured in the balanced tensions of ideological contrasts

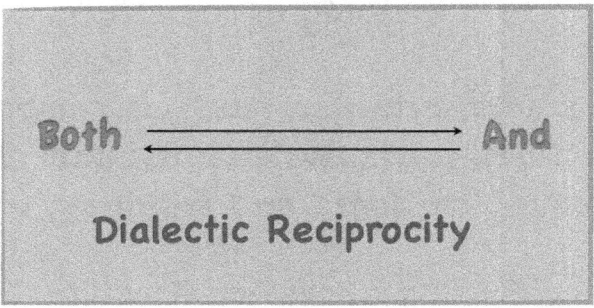

Attached to the top of the framework of a house or building structure is a roof or cover that can repel the elements, and architecturally often serves as the finishing crown to the design and purpose of the structure.

The Finishing Crown

A structure is not finished until it is topped out with a roof or cover.

The top cover repels the elements and is often the finishing crown to the design and purpose of the structure.

The finished crowns of physical buildings can take many different forms.

Topping a Physical Structure

can take many forms

... cupulas, domes ...

towers with spires, and golden domes

and the roofs of our homes

The finishing features of the mentally constructed "House of Christian Contrasts" addresses the practical situations of our Christian experiences as we live life here on earth, and considers how they affect our perspective. Can we rise above the reactions to the "seen" events of life to perceive God's "unseen" perspective of what is transpiring?

The Finishing Features of the Christian Experience

involve the situations of life on earth and how they affect our perspective

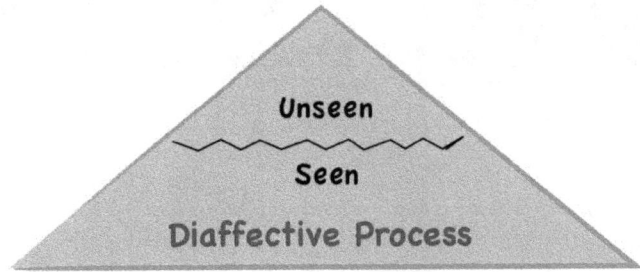

Focusing on the Foundation

With the foregoing overview of the component parts of our conceptual "House of Christian Contrasts" completed, we will now undertake to focus specifically on the foundation of our structure.

As noted previously, the foundation of any building is not the most aesthetic part of the structure. It is often buried underground and not readily visible. Nonetheless, it is fundamentally essential to the integrity of the building.

The foundation of the Christian thought-structure is constructed of the philosophical contrasts of the basic either/ors of spiritual personages or ideological concepts intrinsic to Christian thought.

The Foundation of the Christian Thought-structure

... is constructed of the basic philosophical contrasts of the

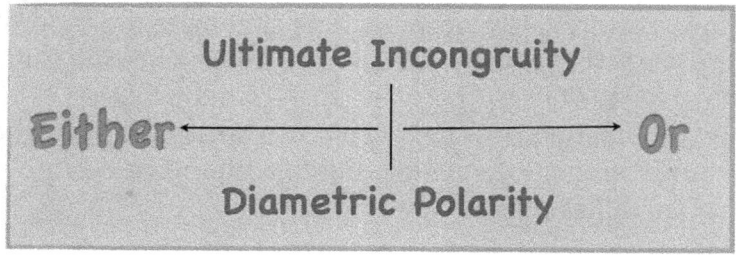

Without a firm foundation built on the bedrock of God's Self-revelation of Himself, we cannot construct a stable Christian theology, much less a stable and consistent Christian life.

The foundational either/ors of Christian thought are incompatible one to the other. They are polar opposites. One pole is as far removed from the other as is possible. There is no middle ground between them; no half way point; no third option or alternative that can be posited as a moderating premise. These two positions cannot be brought together in some kind of merger, amalgamation, fusion, or alliance. There is no neutral ground in between these opposites.

In Aristotelian logic, this is called "the law of the excluded middle," implying that it has to be one or the other; *this* cannot be *that*, and *that* cannot be *this*; and if it is not *this*, then it must be *that*.

It is important to note that these either/or opposites do not create a dualism. There is a separated duality – two separate premises – but not what philosophical thought has termed a "classic dualism." In a "classic dualism" of thought there are opposite equal and eternal forces or powers, neither of which is capable of overcoming the other, resulting in a never-ending stalemate or stand-off. One is not more powerful than the other; one side cannot win over the other; they are forever antagonistic opponents. Dualisms get even more messy when you add a monistic component and end up with the *yin/yang* symbol of Eastern thought.

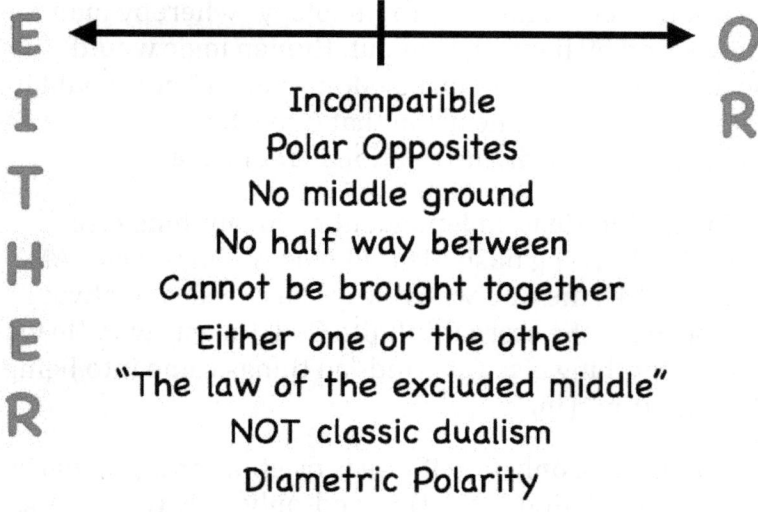

In Christian thought we recognize a "**Diametric Polarity**," but this is not a "dualism" because the Almighty God, Father, Son, and Holy Spirit, is the supreme Being, the sovereign omnipotent Being, who has created all things and living beings, and He can and will subdue and overcome everything that should be opposed to Him. Christian thought is foundationally contrary to all dualistic thought.

We commence, then, with the singularity of the presence and function of the Almighty God. "In the beginning, God..." (Gen. 1:1).

The only things we can know about God are what God has Self-revealed about Himself. We never know about God by natural, human, finite reasoning that expects to discover Him by scientific exploration or by reasoning Him into being by human logic that discovers His attributes. Although there is natural revelation of God in creation, there is no "natural theology" whereby man knows God by figuring Him out. Human logic would never figure out "Trinitarian Monotheism," nor would it ever come to the conclusion that God's Being is comprised of the divine relationality of Love.

God is who He is, independent from anything else. From the burning bush, He told Moses, "I AM who I AM" (Exod. 3:14), the God who always has been, and always will be. He is the eternal-infinite God. He was who He was before anything else was, and "all things came into being through Him" (Jn. 1:3).

What God IS, only God IS! He is original, and singularly one-of-a-kind. God is the One-and-only Holy God, meaning that He is set apart and separated from all that is not Himself. His character is eternally fixed in His own Being. He is "the same yesterday, today, and forever" (Heb. 13:8).

God *does* what He *does* because He IS who He IS. He always acts "in character," expressing His perfect divine character; He never acts out of character. "It is impossible for God to lie" (Heb. 6:18), for example.

As the original and ultimate Being, all other being and beings derive from Him *ek theos* (out of God). The Creator God created other things and other beings, and it appears that the first other beings created were spirit-beings, i.e. angelic-beings. Despite having limited information about their creation and being, the angels were/are choosing creatures, and this necessitated God's Self-limitation of His sovereign control to allow angelic creatures to have "freedom of choice."

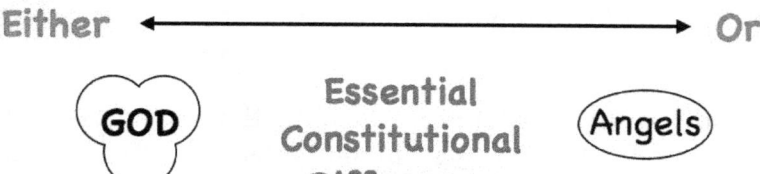

Creator	creature
Divine Being	spirit-being
Intrinsic Being	extrinsic being
Eternal	temporal
Self-generating	derivative being

God, who is Spirit (Jn. 4:24), created spirit-beings who were lesser beings than Himself. He created out of Himself, *ek theos*, creature-beings who were not Himself, i.e. they were not little gods invested with His divine character. There is an "Essential Constitutional Difference" between God and the angels. God is God, and angels are angels!

God is the **Creator** God, the source of everything, the essential cause of all things, but NOT the blame-worthy or culpable cause of evil, which is contrary to His character. The angels were/are creatures, dependent on the Creator. The head of the angelic host was Lucifer, meaning "light-bearer," because he was intended to bear and/or reflect the Light of God.

God is the **Divine Being**, and His being is comprised of the personal relationality of the Father, Son, and Holy Spirit. His Trinitarian Being is not merely comprised of a list of substantive attributes, but of the personal relations of His Triune Being. In contrast, angels are created spirit-beings, not in the same sense that God is Spirit (Jn. 4:24), but not equivalent to human beings either.

God is an **intrinsic Being**, meaning that He exists in and of Himself. He is self-existent, but not self-caused – He did not create Himself. God is the original Being. Angels, on the other hand, have extrinsic being, meaning that their being and existence comes from outside of themselves. They are creatures, and their being was created by God.

God is **eternal** and infinite, beyond space and time. God is everywhere present at every moment. He is omnipresent and eternal. Angels, as created spirit-beings, cannot be everywhere God IS at all times, but neither are they under the same limitations as human beings. They are trans-temporal and trans-locative.

God is Independent and **Self-generating**. He does what He does, because He IS who He IS, and generates His own character in His every action. Angelic creatures, like all creatures, are dependent upon the Creator, and must derive who they are and what they do from the Divine Creator. Angels are derivative beings.

It is here in the foundation of our Christian structure of thought that we see the fundamental truth that differentiates the Creator and the creature, and explains the function of the creature. Creatures are "derivative beings," and not self-generating beings, as only God IS.

We must proceed to explain what happened to Lucifer and the angelic-beings. Lucifer, the head of the heavenly host, was a choosing creature, but his choice was apparently a simple choice, either to say "Yes" to his intended function to reflect the Light of the Creator, or to say "No" and reject his intended function, either to derive from God or to refuse to derive from God. There was not another alternative.

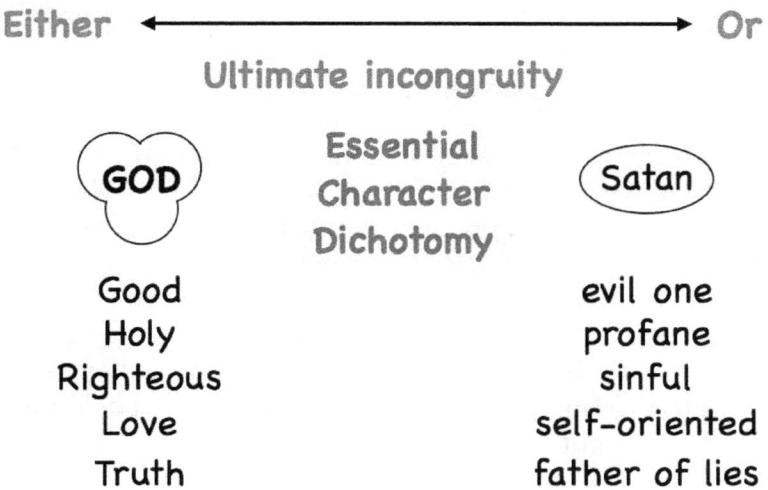

Here, then, we introduce the **"Ultimate Incongruity"** of how Lucifer chose against God the Creator with the selfish assertion, "I will be like the Most High God" (Isa. 14:14). Where did that self-oriented character originate from? It was not derived from God, because God is LOVE for others, and never a Self-for-Self, and He never generates selfish character contrary to who He IS. We are limited to the scant information that is recorded in Isa. 14:12-15; Ezek. 28:11-19; Rev. 12:8,9, and therefore must conjecture *why* and *how* Lucifer could or would have made such a choice. Karl Barth calls it the "impossible possibility."

In the choice that Lucifer made, he became the adversary and enemy of God. He became **Satan**, the Evil One, the Devil, the Destroyer, the very antithesis of God, the fixed negative of God's positive. The question we then ask is, "Did Satan create himself by his own choice of rejection?" How can that be? God is the only Self-generating Being. Even God is not self-caused or self-created! The angels were derivative creatures who of necessity had to derive from another (God) outside of and beyond themselves.

How did Satan come into being? How did evil enter into the good world that God had created? In philosophical theology that question is labeled "theodicy" (*Theos* = God; *dike* = righteousness); how did evil permeate the righteous creation of God? You see why I call this the "Ultimate Incongruity?" Christian thinkers throughout the centuries have never been able to adequately explain the introduction of evil into the perfect created order by the presence of the Evil One.

Now if Lucifer (turned into Satan) was an essentially derivative angelic creature, and must still remain such despite his rejective decision, it would seem that Satan remains a derivative creature, for God is the only Self-generative Being. Does Satan still derive from God, despite his choice to assume God's place? A possible explanation for such might be that Satan takes that which is of God, His divine character, and turns it around backwards to make it come out in opposite form, the reversal of God's intent. He takes what is of God and distorts it, aborts it, misuses and abuses it. This seems to have some justification in Paul's words to Elymas the sorcerer in Acts 13:10, when Paul says, "You son of the devil, you make crooked the straight ways of God."

Despite the limitations of our human explanations, there is an **"Essential Character Dichotomy"** between God and Satan. There is a "diametric polarity" between the absolutely good and perfect character of the Triune

God, and the evil character of the diabolic Evil One. Evil is not merely the privation or absence of God's character, as many have suggested, but there is a personified ontological source of evil that is vested in Satan.

Whereas the character of God is absolute divine perfection, the character of Satan is profane, i.e. godless, impious, always seeking to desecrate, violate and defile the name and character of God.

The character of God is just, righteous, virtuous and loving. God never acts "out of character." The character of the devil, on the other hand, is continuously sinful, wicked, corrupt, nefarious and shameful. Sinful character is anything and everything contrary to the character of God.

"God is LOVE," the apostle John writes twice in I John 4:8,16. Love is always directed toward and concerned for the "other." The opposite of "love" is not "hate," but selfishness, self-oriented character. Remember Lucifer's original declaration of rebellion? "I will be like the Most High God." In becoming Satan, he became the original egoist, the "I" specialist, the self-oriented spiritual source of all selfishness.

God is the "God of Truth," veracity, honesty, integrity. When humans act or speak in truthfulness, their deeds are "wrought in God" (Jn. 3:21). Satan, on the other hand is a "liar, and the father of lies" (Jn. 8:44). He is the "spirit of error" (I Jn. 4:6). In Gen. 2 the devil lied to Adam and Eve.

We move on now to consider another order of beings that have an either/or of diametric polarity.

In the first chapter of Genesis we read that God created the world we live in, and ultimately created mankind, saying, "Let *us* (Father, Son, and Holy Spirit) create man in *our* image" (Gen. 1:26,27).

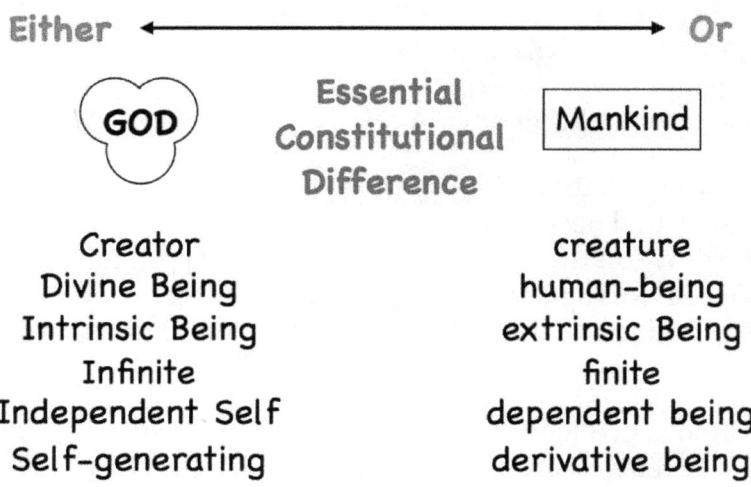

Creator / creature
Divine Being / human-being
Intrinsic Being / extrinsic Being
Infinite / finite
Independent Self / dependent being
Self-generating / derivative being

Again, we see an "Essential Constitutional Difference" between God and mankind. God is God, and man is man. What God is, only God is, and what God does man cannot do, for God does what He does, because He IS who He IS. Soren Kierkegaard called the difference between God and man "the infinite qualitative difference." Karl Barth indicated that God is "wholly other" than man.

The serpent, representing Satan in the garden of Eden, said, "You can be like God." It was a LIE. There is an "essential constitutional difference" between God and man.

God is the **Creator**, the divine Deity who brought all things and all other beings into existence "out of Himself," *ek Theos*, and thereby created human beings, mankind.

Human beings were not meant to be "little gods," nor to become "like God." We are human creatures with an ontological difference of "being." Divine Being and human being are essentially and distinctly different, but God *did* create human creatures with personal, relational capability in order to engage in a personal relationship with the personal Triune God, and with one another.

God has Divine Being, whereas we are human-beings. The angels, you may recall, were/are spirit-beings, and these distinctions of "being" must be kept in mind

Again, we note that God has **intrinsic Being**, meaning that He exists in and of Himself, without any causation from anything or anyone outside of Himself. This does not mean that He is "self-caused," but only that He has eternally existed in and of Himself. Human beings, in distinction, have extrinsic being, meaning that their being or existence comes from outside of themselves, i.e. from the Creator.

God is **infinite**, immeasurable, unlimited, not bounded by space or time. God is omnipotent and omnipresent; all-powerful and everywhere present at the same time. Human beings are limited to space and time. We are uni-temporal and uni-locative. We can only be one place and one time. We noted that angelic spirit-beings are not like God, nor are they like mankind. They seem to be trans-temporal and trans-locative, transcending the singularity of time and place.

God is the only **Independent Self**, complete in Himself, lacking nothing and needing nothing. On the other hand, creatures, both angelic and human, are **not** "independent selves," capable of self-existence or self-function. Humans are dependent beings, dependent on the Creator God to be the human beings we were created to be. What does it take for man to be man as God intended man to be? It takes God in a man for man to be man as God intended man to be! But humanism, the prevailing philosophy of our fallen world, indicates that we have the self-potential to be anything we set our minds to be. Well, that is a LIE (and we know who is the source of all lies, cf. Jn. 8:44). The only truthful antidote to humanism is to realize that the creature-man always depends on God and derives from God to be the human beings we were created to be.

God is **Self-generating**. He *does* what He *does* because He IS who He IS. Human beings, on the other hand, are derivative beings. We cannot generate, manufacture or produce anything out of ourselves. Remember that Jesus said, "Apart from Me, you can *do nothing*" (Jn. 15:5). Human beings always derive character and function from a spiritual source, either God or Satan. We are receivers, not generative doers. This is not passivism. We are responsible to choose our source of derivation. Biblical images always present man as a receiver, as a vessel, branch, house, temple, etc. Human beings always derive their nature, their identity, their character, even their destiny from one spirit-source or the other – God or Satan. (Cf. previous book by Jim Fowler, *Derivative Man: Man as God Intended*. 2017.)

Because God Self-limited Himself to create human beings as choosing creatures with freedom of choice, the option was given to the original human beings, Adam and Eve, to make a choice in the Garden of Eden to eat from the "tree of life," thus deriving from God and allowing for the out-lived life of God in their lives, or to choose from the "tree of the knowledge of good and evil" with the stated consequences of death.

Unlike Lucifer, the original couple had a genuine antithetical choice of two options of derivation, rather than just a "simple choice" of reception or rejection. Present there in the idyllic garden with Adam and Eve were both God and Satan. Satan suggested to the original couple that contrary to God's declaration, they would *not* die if they ate of the tree of the knowledge of good and evil, instead, they would "become like God," capable of being independent, self-generating selves that would not have to derive or depend on God – a definite LIE.

We all know the story, the narrative, of the Fall of mankind into sin in the Garden of Eden. The diametric polarity between **God** and **man** became even more pronounced, more than just the polarity between divine being and human being, but after mankind rejected deriving all life from God there ensued a **"Relational Estrangement and Alienation"** between God and mankind.

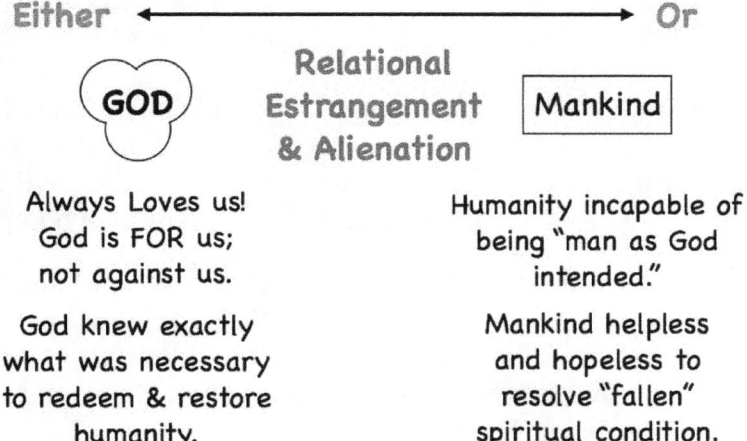

God and man had a personal relationship of spiritual union from the time when God "breathed into man the breath (or Spirit) of life, and man became a living soul" (Gen. 2:7). The in-breathed life of God in man signified the indwelling spiritual presence of God in man, and the tree of life represented the choice to allow God's life to be derivatively lived out in human behavior.

The Fall of man into sin alienated the relationship of man with God. God would not be an unwanted resident in man. He desires only a freely chosen faith/love relationship man. The human race became "alienated from God and hostile in mind toward God" (Col. 1:21), even "enemies" (Rom. 5:10) of God. Since human beings cannot be "independent beings or selves," capable of self-generating their own character-function, the only alternative to God's operative presence in mankind was that Satan usurped the place of God in the spirit of man.

Paul explained to the Ephesians that prior to becoming Christians they were "dead in trespasses and sin," and "the prince of the power of the air (Satan), was the spirit that worked in the sons of disobedience" (Eph. 2:1-3). Spiritual death and the behavioral implications of "dead works" (Heb. 6:1; 9:14) were at work in the human race, for "the one having the power of death, that is the devil" (Heb. 2:14) was in control of God's created human beings.

Many seem to think that God's wrath was poured out on man; that the punitive vengeance of God's anger was directed toward His human creatures, and that He imposed the death consequences upon man. God is not the death-dealer; He is the life-giver!

God is love (I Jn. 4:8,16), and He is always desirous that we be the receptive creatures who exhibit His character unto His own glory. God is always FOR us; not against us! God knew exactly what was necessary to redeem and restore humanity to function as He intended by His presence within man.

Humanity, on the other hand, in their fallen spiritual condition were incapable of being "man as God intended man to be." Still fully human in their fallen condition, mankind was helpless and hopeless to resolve their "fallen" spiritual condition. No amount of self-effort or self-resolve or self-reparation could reconcile man with God again.

God knew what He was going to do from eternity past to redeem and restore the human race to Himself. God was not taken by surprise by man's fall. God is panic-proof, and He never has to revert to "Plan B." In His foreknowledge, He knows the beginning and the end.

God's Grace Initiative to Redeem Man and Restore Man

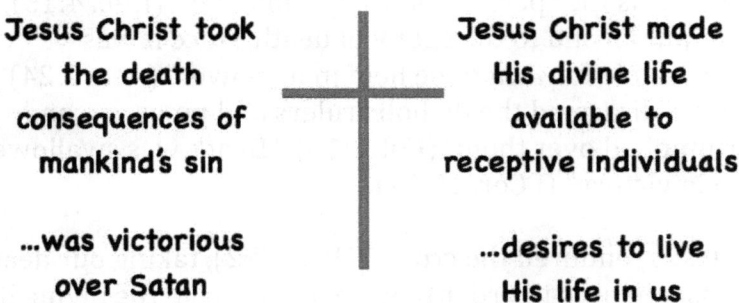

| Jesus Christ took the death consequences of mankind's sin | Jesus Christ made His divine life available to receptive individuals |

...was victorious over Satan   ...desires to live His life in us

As first foretold in the Messianic prophecy of Genesis 3, God was implementing His initiative of GRACE in His Son,

Jesus Christ, to be enacted by the power of His Spirit. Grace is simply God doing what He has determined to do, because He IS who He IS. "God so loved the world (of mankind) that He gave His only begotten Son, that whoever believes in Him should not perish, but have eternal life" (Jn. 3:16

That Son, Jesus, "humbled Himself by becoming obedient unto death, even death on a cross" (Phil. 2:8). That was the purpose of His being sent to earth as "the one Mediator between God and man" (I Tim. 2:5). He "came to give His life a ransom for many" (Matt. 20:28), an "offering for sin" (Rom. 8:3). By His death, Jesus took the death consequences of mankind's sin. In His death, Jesus *incurred* all of the death consequences that had *occurred* in Adam and which were thus transmitted to all mankind, in order to reverse those consequences and allow for spiritual re-creation that man might function as God intended man to function. "He who knew no sin, was made to be sin on our behalf" (II Cor. 5:21).

In submitting to Satan's power of death, Jesus gained the victory over Satan and overcame his power. Because Jesus was the "perfect man," "without sin," (Heb. 4:15), He "put an end to the agony of death, since it was impossible for Him to be held in its power" (Acts 2:24). Jesus "disarmed the diabolic rulers and powers ... and triumphed over them" (Col. 2:15). "Death was swallowed up in victory" (I Cor. 15:54).

Jesus "endured the cross" (Heb. 12:2), taking our death consequences in order that He might make His divine life available to all human individuals who should be receptive to such by faith. "I came that you might have life, and have it more abundantly" (Jn. 10:10), Jesus declared. Eternal life in Jesus Christ is not a futuristic commodity or benefit that Jesus came to dispense. He IS the life He came to give us! "I AM the way, the truth, and the LIFE" (Jn. 14:6), Jesus explained. The apostle John tells us, "He that has the Son has life; he who does not have the Son of God does not have life" (I Jn. 5:12).

The life that Jesus brings in Himself, made individually efficacious when any individual is receptive in faith to receive Him, is not merely a deposit for future benefits. Christ lives in the Christian for the purpose of living His life out through the behavior of the Christian. The Christian life is the re-presentation (more than just a representation) of the life of Jesus Christ. That is why we are called "Christ-ones," Christians. Christ is in us (every Christian), the hope of glory (Col. 1:27), the expectation of manifesting the glorious character of Jesus Christ in all that we do. "The life of Christ is to be manifested in our mortal bodies" (II Cor. 4:10,11). "Christ lives in us, and the life that we now live in the flesh, we live by faith in the Son of God, who loved us and gave Himself for us" (Gal. 2:20). "Christ is our life" (Col. 3:4).

Everything that Jesus Christ was and did in His redemptive ministry on earth was for the purpose of restoring mankind to God's intent, to restore the presence and function of God within the spirit of human individuals.

The life, death, burial, resurrection and ascension of Jesus Christ is the historical prerequisite for the either/or polarity between those who have received the Spirit of Christ and those who continue to function by means of "the spirit that works in the sons of disobedience" (Eph. 2:2).

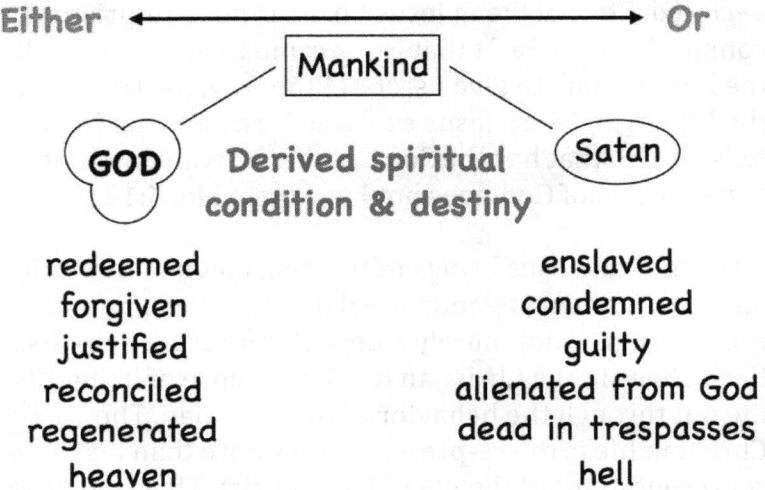

All of **mankind**, that is every human being that now lives, or has ever lived, or will ever live, will of necessity derive their **spiritual condition and destiny** from either **God** or **Satan**. We were created and designed by the Creator God as derivative human creatures, and the only two sources of human spiritual condition and destiny are God or Satan.

Those who respond to the redemptive work of Jesus Christ in faith are **redeemed**. This means that they have been "bought with a price" (I Cor. 6:20; 7:23), and the price paid for their redemption and restoration was the blood of Jesus on the cross (I Pet. 1:18,19). Christians have been "redeemed from the curse of the Law" (Gal. 3:13) and all the performance expectations of religion. The entire price has been paid by Jesus. "We have redemption through His blood" (Eph. 1:7). Without the acceptance of that redemptive action of Jesus, we are **enslaved** to Satan, and "slaves of sin" (Jn. 8:34; Rom. 6:6,17,20; Gal. 4:8; 5:1; Heb. 2:15).

Those who receive the risen and living Lord Jesus into their spirit are **forgiven** of all their sins (Acts 10:43; 26:18; Col. 1:14) and all violation and trespass of the character of God. In addition, the indwelling Spirit of Christ is the Divine Forgiver within the Christian willing and able to forgive anything anyone might do to offend or hurt us. The opposite condition of being forgiven by Christ is to stand condemned to the death consequences that are the only alternative to Christ's forgiveness. Paul explains, "There is now, therefore, *no condemnation* for those who are in Christ Jesus" (Rom. 8:1).

Those who are spiritually united to the living Christ are **justified** and "made righteous." "We are justified as a gift through His grace through the redemption that is in Christ Jesus" (Rom. 3:24). "Having been justified by faith, we have peace with God through our Lord Jesus Christ" (Rom.5:1). Not only do we have a right relationship with God, but we are invested with the very righteousness of Jesus Christ, made spiritually righteous (Rom. 5:19; I Cor. 5:21). Apart from that relationship of spiritual union, every individual stands guilty of rebellion against God and misrepresentation of His character.

Individuals who receive the Spirit of Christ into their spirit are "**reconciled** to God through the death of His Son" (Rom. 5:10). They have a personal relationship with the Triune God, and are no longer alienated from God due to sin.

Christians are **regenerated**, brought into being again with the very life of God in a man. The scripture calls this regenerative action "being born again" (Jn. 3:3,7; I Pet. 1:23). "By His great mercy God has caused us to be born again to a living hope through the resurrection of Jesus from the dead" (I Pet. 1:3). Only by such "new birth" does an individual avoid being spiritually dead in trespasses and sin (Eph. 2:1,5), along with the extended death consequence of everlasting death.

The polarity of our destiny is perpetuated in the contrasts of the extension of spiritual life or death in **heaven or hell**. Jesus had much to say about the presence of God in the "kingdom of heaven." In fact, Paul explained that Christians are even now seated in the heavenly places (Eph. 1:3; 2:6). But those who remain in their fallen and sinful spiritual condition must face the alternative possibility of being cast into "the unquenchable fire" (Mk. 9:43) of a protracted "hell" (Mk. 9:45,47).

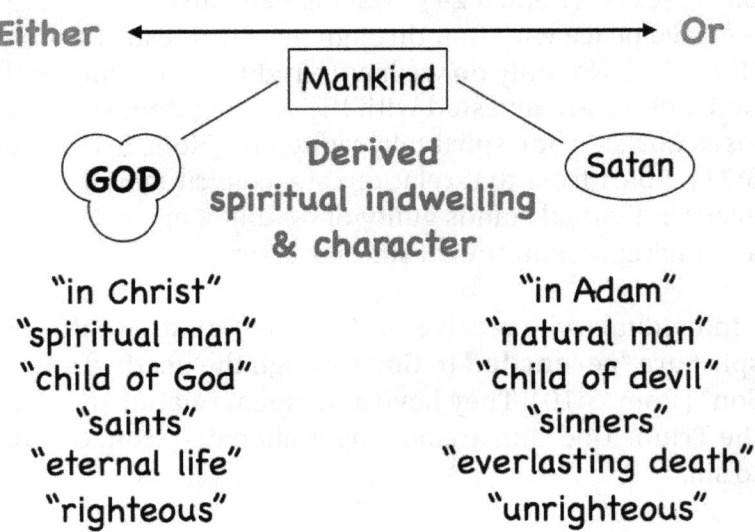

The contrasts of one's derived spiritual condition allow us to see that human beings are spiritually indwelt by the spiritual personages of either God or Satan, and derive character from one or the other.

An individual is either **"in Christ,"** the Savior, or **"in Adam,"** the disobedient transgressor; identified with one representative man or the other (cf. Rom. 5:12-21). Those are the only two spiritual families that we can be associated with. Paul states the contrast clearly in I Cor. 15:22 - "*in Adam* all die; whereas *in Christ* all are made alive." Also, "If any man is in Christ, he is a new creature; old things have passed away, behold all things (spiritual) have been made new" (II Cor. 5:17). To be "in Christ" is to have spiritual union with the Spirit of Christ, and to be made part of the Body of Christ on earth, the Church. Christians have been "baptized into Christ Jesus, and have clothed ourselves with Christ" (Gal. 3:27), and are "baptized into one Body (the Church) and made to drink of one Spirit (the Spirit of Christ) (I Cor. 12:13).

Those who have received the Spirit of Christ into their spirit become Christians, and that, by the way, is the only way to become a Christian. "If any man does not have the Spirit of Christ, he is none of His" (i.e. not a Christian)- (Rom. 8:9). But having received the Spirit of Christ, "the Spirit bears witness with our spirit that we are sons of God" (Christians) - (Rom. 8:16). Every person who has the Spirit of Christ as a Christian, is identified as a **"spiritual man,"** for this designation does not refer to someone who has achieved some criteria of "spirituality" (as determined by a religious group). A Spirit indwelt and Spirit-filled Christian is a "spiritual man." The unregenerate, non-Christian person is identified as a **"natural man."** "The natural man cannot understand spiritual things, for they are spiritually appraised" (I Cor. 2:14). The "natural man" has only a wisdom that is earthly, natural and demonic" (James 3:15).

The apostle John, who specializes in the either/or contrasts, explains that "the **children of God** and the **children of the devil** are obvious" (I John 3:10). "As many as received Him (Jesus Christ), God the father gave the right to be called "children of God," even to those who believe in His name" (Jn. 1:12). Those who have not received the Spirit of Christ are "of their father, the devil" (Jn. 8:44), as Jesus explained to the religious leaders of Israel.

The unregenerate have a spiritual identity of "**sinners**." This is not a designation based on their sinful behavior, but is a spiritual identity formulated by the Satanic source of all sin, Satan, dwelling in all fallen mankind. "By one man's disobedience (Adam's sin in the Garden) the many (that is all humanity) were *made sinners*" (Rom. 5:19). And "God demonstrated His love toward us, in that while we were yet sinners, Christ died for us" (Rom. 5:8). When we receive Jesus Christ, we cease to be "sinners" and become "saints." Again, this is not based on our performance, but is a spiritual identity based on the presence of the Holy One, Jesus, dwelling in us. Every Christian is a saint, a "holy one," because Jesus, the Holy One, dwells in him or her.

The Christian has **"eternal life**," the presence of the Person of the Living Savior, rather than the **"everlasting death"** that is the perpetuity of the non-Christian's identification with the "one having the power of death, that is the devil" (Heb. 2:14).

"The **unrighteous** will not inherit the kingdom of God" (I Cor. 6:9), but those who have been "made righteous" (Rom. 5:19; I Cor. 5:21) by the indwelling presence of the Righteous One (Acts 3:14; 7:52; 22:14), Jesus Christ. We are "**righteous**," not by our righteous deeds, but it is a spiritual identity based on the spiritual identity and character of Jesus Christ, the Righteous One, living in us.

To conclude our consideration of the diametric polarity of the either/or contrasts that are foundational to Christian thought, we will switch to the diagram of **concentric circles** that many are quite familiar with. Using two-dimensional concentric circles, we attempt to illustrate the various levels wherein God designed the human person to function.

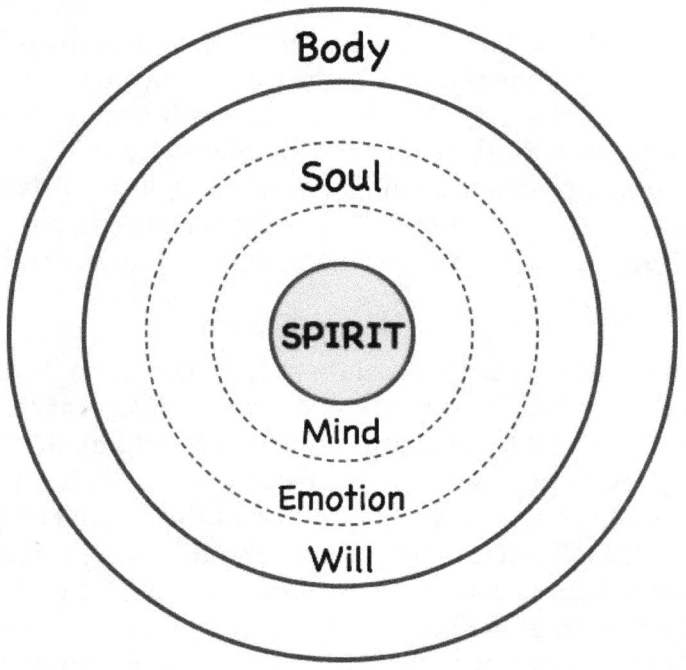

At the core of his being, a human being has **spiritual** function. This is not an inherent or intrinsic or independent spiritual function. (Man is not an "independent self.") It is a spiritual function wherein we have the capacity to be occupied by a spiritual personage, either the Spirit of Christ or the spirit of the Evil One in our human spirit, and to derive spiritual character from the spirit that formulates our spiritual nature and identity.

We also have psychological function in our soul. The Greek word for "soul" is *psuche*, from which we get the words "psyche" and "psychology." Psychological function pertains to mental, emotional, and volitional function in the human mind, emotions and will.

External behavioral function of the human being is manifested in the physical body. Unlike the old Greek philosophy that regarded the human body as merely a prison-house for the soul, with an inherently evil character and orientation, Christian thought regards the human body as an important agency of expressing the derived spiritual character that dwells within the spirit of a man.

This tri-level function of humanity is evident in Paul's statement, "Now may the God of peace Himself sanctify you entirely (set you apart to function as intended at every level), and may your **spirit and soul and body** be preserved complete, without blame at the coming of our Lord Jesus Christ" (I Thess. 5:23). The following verse is also important: "Faithful is He who calls you; He will bring it to pass" (I Thess. 5:24). Proper human function at all levels is not achieved by the performance of human self-effort, but only as God the Father in Christ, and by the Spirit work within us from the inside out. Heb. 4:12 is another relevant verse: "The word of God (that is the living Lord Jesus, not a book) pierces as far as the division of soul and spirit, and is able to judge the thoughts and intentions of the heart." The indwelling Jesus knows that the natural thoughts of man in the psychological mind must be distinguished and differentiated from the spiritual intents of our hearts, wherein every Christian desires at the deepest level to be a godly man or woman.

The natural spiritual condition of every person since the Fall of Adam and Eve into sin by their disobedience in the Garden, involves being born with the wrong spirit in the core of our being. Paul explained to the Ephesians, "the prince of the power of the air (the devil), was the **spirit** working in the sons of disobedience" (Eph. 2:2). The need of every human person is to be converted "from darkness to light, from the dominion of Satan to the dominating control of the Spirit of God" (Acts 26:18). Thus, we can refer to the spiritual exchange wherein the **Spirit of Christ** comes to dwell in the spirit of a receptive Christian.

In that God and Satan are incompatible, as evidenced by the either/or polarity we have been noting, the "**spirit**" of the Evil One must depart and go into exile, subsequently functioning as the **Satanic tempter**, the "accuser of the brethren" (Rev. 12:10), hurling "fiery darts" (Eph. 6:16) over the wall into our lives.

Christians must always remember, "Greater is He who is in you (Jesus Christ), than he who is in the world" (I Jn. 4:4).

EXAMINING THE FRAMEWORK

We have previously noted that our conceptual "House of Christian Contrasts" has philosophical contrasts, ideological contrasts, and experiential contrasts, and these comprise the various levels of the structure.

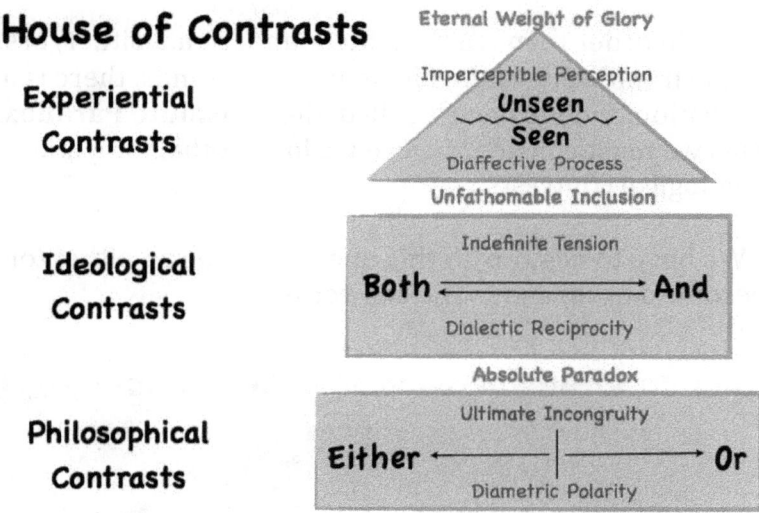

The philosophical or theological contrasts are seen in the foundation of the either/ors, the diametric polarities, wherein one must address the "ultimate incongruity" of the introduction of evil into God's good and righteous creation.

The ideological or conceptual contrasts comprise the framework of the both/ands, wherein the dialectic reciprocity of differing doctrinal themes, topics and tenets must be maintained in "indefinite tension" of Christian thinking.

The practical and experiential contrasts are built into the "seen" versus "unseen" distinction, wherein we engage in the diaffective process of moving beyond our immediate natural reactions to the experiences of life in order to behold the "unseen" dimension with an "counter-intuitive perception" that is the privilege of the Christian who is in union with God in Christ.

But, in order to move from the foundational either/ors to the framework of the ideological both/ands, there is a transition that we have labelled, the "**Absolute Paradox.**" This we must consider before we look at the both/and ideological contrasts.

We have to begin with this question: "Can an either/or become a both/and?" The answer is NO!

Can an **either/or** become a **both/and?** NO!

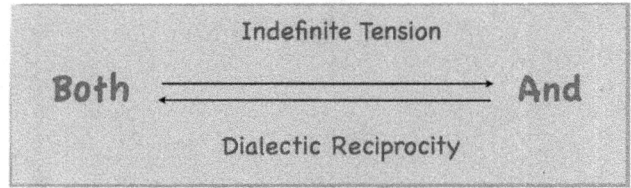

Absolute Paradox

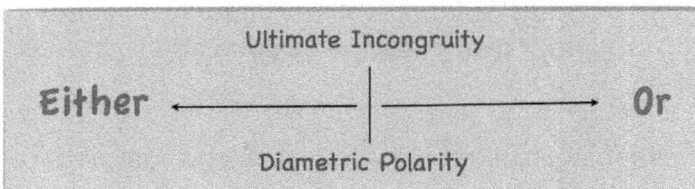

The diametric polarity of the either/ors cannot be logically converted into the dialectic reciprocity of ideological both/ands. It is a logical impossibility – a logical absurdity.

Remember what we said about the either/or contrasts: The either/or personages and theses stand in opposition to one another, allowing for no convergence, conjunction, merging, fusing, amalgamation, or bringing them together in a combined alliance. They stand alone in isolated apposition to the alternative opposite. The opposites in the either/or categories are antithetical to each other. They are incompatible. They push against each other and repel each other like the opposite sides of two magnets.

The either/ors are polar opposites with diametric polarity pushing them apart. They are as far removed the one from the other as far-apart can be. There is no middle ground between them, no half way point, no third option or alternative that can be posited as a moderating premise. *This* cannot be *that*, and *that* cannot be *this*. The Greek philosopher, Aristotle, called this "the law of the excluded middle."

There can be no synthesis to the either/or premises. Eastern religion attempts to do so in the *yin/yang* principles, for example, but all they end up with is a monistic morass of confusion.

Can you imagine trying to put God and Satan into a singular category? They are adamant antagonists, adversaries, absolutely incompatible. They represent the positive versus the negative.

God and man are equally opposite from one another. The Creator-God and the creature-man are "wholly other." There is an "essential constitutional difference" between deity and humanity, as well as an "essential functional difference" between the two. Though both kinds of "being" are capable of personal relationship, the human race was estranged and alienated from God in the Fall of man into sin. Fallen mankind are said to be "enemies" (Rom. 5:10) of God.

Is it conceivable that this dichotomy between man and God could be neutralized and homogenized into an emulsified entity? Human logic does not allow for such!

Is it possible that the eternal/infinite God outside of space and time could be limited and temporal inside space and time?

Is it possible that the infinite God could become finite?

Is it possible for the intrinsic "Being" of God to be transformed into the extrinsic "being" of a human being?

Is it possible that the invisible God, whom "no man has seen at any time" (I Tim. 6:16) could become visible?

Can an immortal God become mortal? Can the Creator-God become a limited creature? Can the God who is Spirit (Jn. 4:24) become flesh? Such a nexus and joining together of God and man is an inconceivable contradiction according to human logic?

Swiss theologian, Karl Barth, called it an "impossible possibility." The Danish thinker, Soren Kierkegaard, indicated that the "Absolute Paradox," explaining that God and man becoming a God-man in the Person of Jesus Christ was beyond all human reason. It was an absolutely singular and unique event, a once and for all interpenetration of God into space and time, allowing for the joining of the Son of God into a singular and unique divine-human Person, the God-man.

Only God in His infinite Theo-logic and with His inexhaustible divine Power could even conceive of and enact such a coming together of God and man.

We could call this the "ultimate paradox" or the "incomprehensible paradox," but Kierkegaard's designation works quite well.

"Absolute Paradox"
Soren Kierkegaard

Ultimate Paradox
Incomprehensible Paradox

Incarnational Conundrum

What is a "paradox? anyway?

One wit suggested that when you see a cardiologist and an endocrinologist standing together having a discussion on the second floor of the local hospital, there you have a "pair of docs." Humorous, perhaps, but a paradox is a logical conundrum, wherein two seemingly contradictory tenets, regarded to be in abeyance and apposition to one another are brought together in the tensioned positioning of a simultaneous relative consideration of the two. In the case of Jesus Christ becoming the God-man, it is the cosmic, universal and absolute paradox of all human thought.

"God so loved the world that He gave His only begotten Son" (Jn. 3:16), and "the Word (the Son of God) became flesh and dwelt among us" (Jn. 1:14). "Although He existed in the form of God, He did not regard equality with God a thing to be held on to, but emptied Himself, taking the form of a bond-servant, being made in the likeness of men" (Phil. 2:6,7).

Christians are sometimes so familiar with the story of the human birth of the baby Jesus, consenting to the theological implication of the incarnation of the Son of God in a man, that we often do not realize how "out of the ordinary" and "beyond all human comprehension" the Christmas story, the historical birth of the God-man, Jesus, really is!

We will never fully understand the supernatural miracle of how the Son of God became a human being in Jesus Christ. The early Christians pondered this imponderable event, and their best explanation, drafted at the Council of Chalcedon in A.D. 451, was that there was an indivisible and indissoluble hypostatic union of deity and humanity in the one Person of Jesus, whereby He was fully God and fully man; never less than God, never more than man. This may be an acceptable human explanation, but the event remains an "absolute paradox."

It is the "incarnational conundrum" of the God-man being born as a baby boy in the manger in Bethlehem – the Lord and King of the universe sought by the Magi following the star.

We return now to constructing our "House of Christian Contrasts" and attempt to "frame" our thinking by looking at the "dialectic reciprocity" of the both/ands, knowing that we will have to live with the "indefinite tension" of a personal uncertainty wherein we can never get our doctrinal definitions down-pat and absolutized in a way that will be acceptable to all our Christian brethren.

Oh, how we want to get everything figured out with our finite minds, and then seek to categorize and systematize the subject at hand, thinking that we can "nail down" the truth, get a handle on the truth, and take great pride in being knowledgeable Christians.

The word "dialectic" comes from two Greek words: *dia* = through; *lectos* = to talk (ex. English word "lecture"). Dialectic means "to talk through," to dialogue between two different words or ideas, to allow those words or ideas to "talk back and forth" reciprocally, and bounce off of each other. Dialectic involves a constant and continual conversational interaction of contrasting concepts.

In a previous study, published in book form as *Two Sides of Every Coin: A Dialectic Formatting of Christian Thought*, a more complete perusal of the interactive both/ands within Christian categories was considered than will be possible in the brief confines of this study.

Two Sides of Every Coin

The two sides of a particular coin, however, does not adequately illustrate the both/and of dialectics. The two sides of a coin are an either/or. We flip the coin and it lands *either* "heads" *or* "tails."

There are other illustrations that more adequately represent the back and forth balance of dialectic reciprocity:

The balance scale, sometimes referred to as a "scale of justice," represents a two-sided balance, but once the weights are placed in each tray, there is no more movement and it becomes a static balance; it is not moving in a continuous reciprocity.

The process of learning to ride a bicycle does have a dynamic sense of balance. You cannot ride a bicycle unless you keep moving, and you are constantly adjusting the handlebars one direction or the other to keep your balance.

My wife and I had four daughters, and they were all competitive gymnasts for differing lengths of time. One of the dreaded events in women's gymnastics is the "balance beam." There is a definite sense of dynamic balance as the girls attempt to do ever more difficult tricks and tumbling while standing, running, jumping and flipping on that narrow beam. Points are deducted for failure to keep your balance.

But the illustration that I think best represents the concept of dialectic reciprocity, is the tree swing that I constructed in the backyard for our grandchildren. The pivot-point is at the top where the ropes are attached to the tree limb, allowing the child on the swing seat to be pushed back and forth. "Push me Papa ... harder ... faster ... higher." We even set the above-ground swimming pool in front of the swing so they could swing out and jump in the pool at the high point of the forward swing. That, however, takes a precise sense of timing to let go and jump at the correct time, and we soon recognized that though it was great fun, it could be quite dangerous. So that practice was suspended, much to the dismay of the grandchildren.

"Push me Papa – harder ... faster ... higher"

Back and forth, back and forth, the grandchildren would swing, until Papa was tired of pushing.

One thing they did not like was to merely sit on the swing when it was not moving – when it was static. There was no fun in sitting on the swing as it hung in the dead center position. They wanted the dynamic motion of the reciprocity of going as high as they could in each direction.

The following diagram illustrates the dynamic balance of interactive dialectic reciprocity.

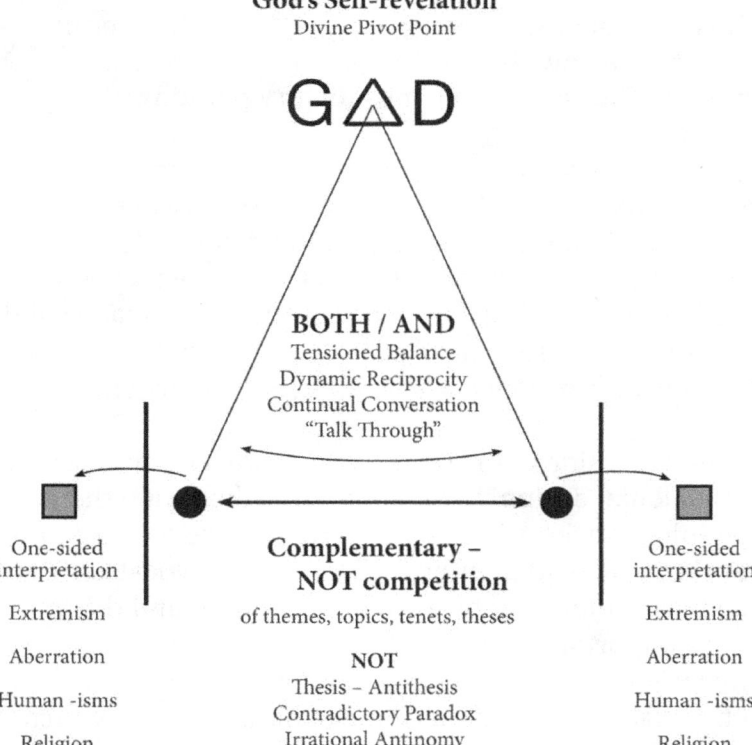

God is the pivot-point of the dynamic movement back and forth of Christian dialectic ideas. Two ideas that are placed in juxtaposition with one another have a tensioned balance whereby they go back and forth in dynamic reciprocity, continually "talking through" the dialectic of their both/and veracity. The two themes, topics, tenets, or theses are not in competition with one another, but are complementary. Both tenets of the dialectic find their source in the revelation of God. In accord with His scriptures, God has declared that both themes are true.

It is necessary that they bounce off of each other in order to see how they coexist in tension with one another. They are not a contradictory paradox.

Just as the grandchildren were not happy to sit in the middle "dead center" position on the tree swing, so it is that we must not seek to find a middle point of synergistic compromise between the two tenets being considered. They must both be accepted as equally valid truth-tenets revealed by God, and be allowed to engage in dynamic interplay, like a syncopated counterpoint.

When one side of the equation, one idea is emphasized to the denial or diminishment of the other, then the pendulum sticks up against one wall or the other, and we develop a one-sided interpretation that advocates that one idea is more important than the other, and the other is less important, or just not true. These one-sided interpretations that lose sight of the dynamic reciprocity of the dialectic, lead to extremism or aberration, which are all too common in religious thinking in every generation. In fact, entire denominations are formed when people decide to camp out on one side or the other.

BOTH / AND
Dialectic Charts

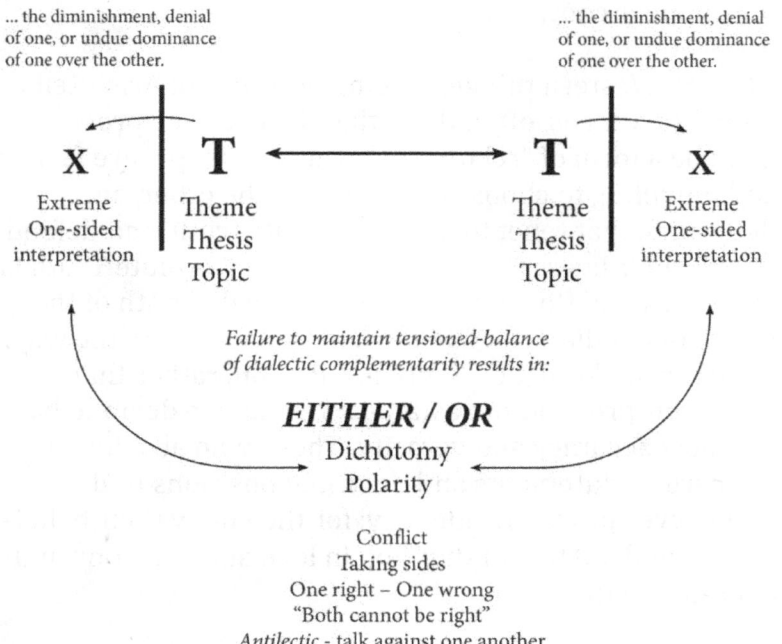

Continuing to diagram and illustrate the necessity of dialectic reciprocity where two themes, theses or topics are maintained in the tensioned-balance of complementarity, we note again that the diminishment, neglect or denial of one truth-tenet, allowing the other to dominate, leads to the extremism of a one-sided interpretation, elevating one idea to supremacy over the other revealed truth.

It is tragic that Christians (and groups of Christians) have so often allowed the pendulum to stick on one side or the other of the dialectic. We have this tendency in the Western world to think that we should pick one idea over the other, that it must be *this* or *that*; it can't be both at the same time, especially when there are times when they appear contradictory.

In fact, Western thinkers, being products of Aristotelian thought patterns, often think that dialectic reciprocity must be a form of "relativism," wherein people are fearful and unwilling to choose one thesis or the other, and determine that tenet to be the absolute truth, and defend it with their lives. They need to see that Absolute Truth is in the Being of God alone, who has revealed both of the tenets of the dialectic dilemma. Jesus said, "I AM the way, the truth, and the life." Truth is a Person, rather than particular propositional statements that we deem to have the most accuracy and veracity. Those who absolutize their truth-statements and doctrinal positions find themselves practicing idolatry, for they deify their belief-system and fail to worship God in love and harmony and open-mindedness.

When individuals or groups develop a one-sided fundamentalist mind-set, then they encounter persons or groups who have taken the opposite position emphasizing the premise on the other side, and they polarize in order to engage in sanctified Christian warfare. NO, there is nothing sanctified about the conflict that ensues when Christian people and groups take sides, believing that their side is "right" and the other side "wrong," because "both sides cannot be right." They have sacrificed the divine dialectics of both/and tension, and instead engage in "antilectic," talking against one another.

There is such a need in Christian circles to maintain the balance of dialectic thought, to see the truths of God stereoscopically without becoming double-minded. We need to allow diverse ideas to *complete* each other, rather than *compete* against each other.

"My thoughts are not your thoughts, neither are your ways My ways," declares the Lord. "For as the heavens are higher than the earth, so are My ways higher than your ways, and My thoughts than your thoughts" (Isa. 55:8,9).

We will be taking a look at some dialectic charts that demonstrate the reciprocity of both/and dialectic balance with the "indefinite tension" that exists between the tenets. We will commence with charts that deal with Jesus Christ, for Christian thought must maintain a Christocentric understanding.

BOTH ⇌ AND
Jesus Christ

	God	Man	
Docetism Greek dokein "to appear" –Jesus only "appeared to be human."	Deity, Divinity Son of God Jn. 1:1 - "Word was God" Phil. 2:6 - "existed in the form of God" Col. 2:9 - "in Him fulness of deity dwells"	Humanity Son of Man Acts 2:22 - "a man" Rom. 5:15 - "the One Man, Jesus Christ" Phil. 2:8 - "found in appearance as a man"	Radical Kenoticism Jesus emptied himself of divinity.
Absorptionism humanity of Jesus was absorbed or subsumed into deity.	Titus 2:13 - "God and Savior, Christ Jesus"	I Tim. 2:5 - "the man, Christ Jesus	Adoptionism Jesus just a man adopted by God and given Messiah mantle or Christ-cloak.

Hypostatic Union

The Council of Chalcedon (A.D. 451) explained that the two natures (divine and human) were united into one personal individual, the God-man, Jesus Christ.

The dialectic of Jesus Christ as the God-man is central to Christian thought. The revelation of God is clear, as recorded in the inspired scriptures, that the Person of Jesus Christ was simultaneously both God and man. The Son of God "existed in the form of God" (Phil. 2:6) and "was God" (John 1:1), and "became flesh" (John 1:14), "found in appearance as a man" (Phil. 2:8), "the man, Christ Jesus" (I Tim. 2:5). At the Council of Chalcedon in A.D. 451, church thinkers explained that "two natures, divine and human, were united into one personal individual, the God-man, Jesus Christ."

When the deity of Jesus is emphasized to the neglect of His humanity, then aberrant and heretical opinions ensue. The first heresy of the early church was Docetism, the idea that Jesus was God, but only appeared (Greek word *dokein*) to be human.

When the humanity of Jesus is emphasized to the neglect or denial of His deity, aberrant and heretical opinions are formulated in the opposite ditch. Adoptionism was another second century heresy that attempted to explain that Jesus was just a human being who was "adopted" by God, and was given the "Messiah mantle" or "Christ-cloak" to represent Himself as the divinized human savior.

As difficult as it might be to explain with human logic, the revelation of God indicates that Jesus Christ is both divine and human. Any attempts to emphasize one over the other, or one to the diminishment of the other, will result in aberrant opinions. We must hold the two premises of His deity and humanity together in dialectic tension if we are to maintain genuine Christian teaching.

BOTH ⇌ AND
Jesus Christ

	Savior	Lord	
Easy-believism Revivalism - get people down the aisle to "get saved" - salvation is a pass into heaven - spiritual fire-insurance policy - "off the hook"	Jesus was incarnated to deliver humanity from sin and to "make them safe." Matt. 1:21 - "He will save people from their sins" John 4:42 - "this One is the Savior of the world" Titus 1:4 - "Christ Jesus our Savior." I Jn. 4:14 - "the Father sent the Son to be the Savior of the world" I Tim. 2:4 - "desires all men to be saved"	Jesus came to be the divine authority over mankind and God's creation Matt. 28:18 - "all authority given to Me. in heaven and on earth." Acts 2:36 - "God has made Him both Lord and Christ." Rom. 10:9 - "if confess Jesus as Lord, you will be saved." Phil. 2:11 - "every tongue will confess that Jesus Christ is Lord."	Lordship Salvation Ethical Behaviorism Pietism that inspects performance as test of salvation and obedience. - "fruit-inspectors" Demand for obedience.

Another both/and dialectic referring to Jesus Christ is the recognition that Jesus is, and functions as, both Savior and Lord.

The intent of the redemptive mission of the Son of God was that He would "save the people from their sins" (Matt. 1:21), and be the "Savior of the world" (Jn. 4:42). At the same time, He was to exercise authority over mankind and all creation, serving as the divine Lord.

When these two functions of Jesus' Being are not kept in balance, misguided emphases become evident. Some Christians have emphasized the saving activity of Jesus to the neglect of His Lordship, by extending a revivalistic "easy-believism" that seeks only to "get people saved" in order to escape the disastrous destiny of hell. On the other hand, some Christians have advocated a "Lordship salvation" that focuses on particular pious behavior as proof of one's salvation. Both of these emphases need to maintain the reciprocity of Jesus' being Savior and Lord.

Jesus Christ
BOTH ⇌ AND

	Physical Jesus	Pneumatic Jesus	
Jesus just a person who lived 2000 years ago. Scholars seek "historical Jesus" Church is but "historical society" for remembrance of Jesus.	Historical Jesus Incarnated Jesus Jn. 1:14 - "the Word became flesh" Rom. 8:3 - "God sent His Son in the likeness of sinful flesh..." I Tim. 3:16 - "He was revealed in the flesh, and vindicated in the Spirit" Heb. 2:14 - "He Himself partook of flesh and blood	Spiritual Jesus Experiential Jesus I Cor. 15:45 - "the Last Adam became the life-giving Spirit. Rom. 1:4 - "Spirit of holiness, Jesus our Lord" II Cor. 3:17 - "Lord is the Spirit" I Cor. 6:17 - "joined to Lord, one spirit with Him Rom. 8:9 - "do not have Spirit of Christ, none of His"	Some indicate it is inconsequential whether Jesus ever lived as an historical person. Jesus viewed only as Spirit-being mystically related to the spirit...

    A third both/and dialectic concerning Jesus Christ is the necessary recognition that He was both the historically incarnated Jesus and the experiential spiritual Jesus who continues to live as the risen Christ.

    Historically, the Son of God was physically incarnated in the womb of the virgin Mary, and was "made in the likeness of men" (Phil. 2:7), partaking of "flesh and blood" (Heb. 2:14). The same Jesus, raised from the dead in resurrection, "became the life-giving Spirit" (I Cor. 15:45), the "Spirit of holiness, Jesus our Lord" (Rom. 1:4).

    If one emphasizes the physical "historical Jesus," without recognizing the continuing pneumatic Spirit of Christ, the dynamic function of the living Christ is diminished. The opposite extreme of disregarding the historicity of Jesus' redemptive life on earth, and focusing only on Jesus as a mystical "Spirit-being," likewise leads to an unbalanced aberration that fails to maintain the both/and of Jesus' action in both the past and present.

BOTH ⇌ AND

God

	One Being	Three Persons	
Mathematical oneness – one integer Monad mono-thesism – Unextended unit of ONE – Jehovah – Allah Monistic – god in all things Unitarianism	Unity, simplicity, singular One Supreme God (Deut. 6:4; I Cor. 8:6; Eph. 4:6 Monotheism – one nature, essence, being Council of Nicea – AD 325 Father, Son, Holy Spirit are one homoousian – same Being in relation. Gregory of Nazianzus – perichoresis – triune persons interpenetrate each other. Jn. 14:10,11 – "I in the Father and Father in Me"	Plurality, multiplicity Father, Son, Holy Spirit – co-equal, co-essential John 10:30 – " I and the Father are one." – Jewish leaders thought this was blasphemy. Christians are obliged to explain the Trinity. Council of Nicea – AD 325 3 hypostases – Greek particulars, distinct 3 personae – Latin persons Tertullian – trinitas Latin	Tritheism – 3 gods – polytheism Plurality? heteroousion – different anomoousion – not same homoiousion – similar Subordination-ism – Spirit & Son inferior Modalism

At the heart of the Christian understanding of God is the distinctive awareness of Trinitarian monotheism. God is three Persons, Father, Son and Holy Spirit, in one Divine Being. This dialectic has befuddled both unbelievers and believers through the centuries.

A monotheistic god was the heritage of the Hebrew peoples. "The Lord our God is one Lord" (Deut. 6:4). Jesus stretched that monotheistic thought when He said, "I and the Father are one" (Jn. 10:30), and we interpenetrate one another, "I am in the Father, and the Father is in Me" (Jn. 14:10,11). The Jewish leaders considered such a statement to be blasphemy. The Christian council of Nicea declared that the divine Father and Son were *homoousion* (the same Being).

If the oneness of God's Being is stressed to the neglect of the plurality of Persons, a monadic or monistic monotheism results. If the Threeness of God is emphasized over His Oneness, this can result in a form of tritheism (three gods) or a reductionism of modalism.

BOTH ⇌ AND
God

	Transcendent	Immanent	
Deism - God is distant, removed, separated. God is: - "up there" - "wholly other" God not in control of universe. Gnosticism - God is untouchable	Above & beyond creation. Beyond space and time. In a class by Himself - distinct from all else. - independent - autonomous qualitative difference Isa. 57:15 - "high and exalted One." Jere. 23:23 - "a god who is far off" Ps. 113:5 - "God enthroned on high." Worthy of worship, awe, and reverence.	Involved and present in space/time creation God is close and near. In creation: Col. 1:17 - "in Him all things consist." Ps. 139:7 - "where can I flee from Your presence?" In new creation: Jn. 1:14 - "the Word became flesh" I Jn. 4:12,15,16 - "God abides in us" Col. 1:27 - "Christ in us"	Pantheism Monism Immanentism - God not distinguished from creation Humanization of God - God is in every man - "God is my buddy" Mysticism

    The Triune God of Christian thought is both transcendent above and beyond the space and time wherein human beings exist, as well as immanently involved and present in the space/time creation He created.

    The Christian God is "enthroned on high" (Ps. 113:5), "high and exalted" (Isa. 57:15), and the Son of God is "seated at the right hand of the Father" (Acts 2:33), worthy of worship, awe and reverence. At the same time, God is invested in His creation, and the Son of God indwells and abides in those who are Christians (Gal. 2:20; Col. 1:27; I Jn. 4:12,15,16).

    To emphasize the transcendence of God apart from His immanence tends to lead to a deistic concept where God is detached and separated from His creation and the people with whom He wants personal relationship. To emphasize the immanence of God without balancing with His transcendence can lead to various forms of pantheism and mystical oneness.

BOTH ⇌ AND
Holy Spirit

	Fruit of Spirit	Gifts of Spirit	
Fruit of Spirit viewed as detached elements to be achieved.	Character of Christ Gal. 5:22,23 - "fruit of Spirit is love, joy, peace, patience, kindness, goodness, faithfulness, gentleness, self-control.	Ministry of Christ Rom. 12:6-8 - "gifts that differ, prophecy, service, teaching, exhortation, giving, leading, showing mercy."	Gifts of Spirit viewed as personal possessions, or trophies of spirituality.
Fruit of Spirit viewed as productivity results of evangelistic endeavors.	Provision of Spirit to express character of Christ in our behavior. Matt. 7:16,20 - "you will know them by fruit" Christians known by their expression of love. Eph. 5:19; Phil. 1:11 - "fruit of righteousness"	Provision of Spirit to express ministry of Christ in the Church. Functionality in Body of Christ is based on our spiritual giftedness to the needs of local church and the world around us.	Gifts of Spirit viewed as "power tools" of supernatural activity.

As the third Person of the Godhead, the Holy Spirit is co-equal and co-essential with the Father and the Son. By the Spirit's indwelling in the human spirit of receptive persons God immanently manifests His character and ministry through human creatures.

The character of Christ is manifested in Christians by the "fruit of the Spirit," listed by Paul as "love, joy, peace, patience, kindness, goodness, faithfulness, gentleness and godly control of oneself" (Gal. 5:22,23). Jesus' disciples will be "known by their fruit" (Matt. 17:16,20) of righteous character (cf. Eph. 5:19; Phil. 1:11). The functional ministry of Christ in the Body of Christ is expressed via the "gifts of the Spirit" (Rom. 12:6-8).

If the *being* of spiritual character in the "fruit of the Spirit" is separated from the *doing* of spiritual ministry via the "gifts of the Spirit," Christians can become but an enclave of interactive kindness. Employing the "gifts of the Spirit" apart from the character of Christ produces but a beehive of religious busyness.

BOTH ⇌ AND

Salvation

	Grace	Faith	
Augustine Calvinism - Humans incapable of response to God's grace. - Grace is determinism: God elects some to be saved, and others to be damned.	Divine Initiative Eph. 2:5,8 - "for by grace are you saved…" Grace is dynamic of God's action in Jesus Christ. Acts 15:11 - "saved through grace of Jesus" Titus 2:11-grace appeared bringing salvation to all men." II Tim. 1:9-"saved according to His purpose and grace."	Human Response Eph. 2:8 - "saved through faith" Faith is human receptivity to God's activity. Acts 16:31 - "believe in Jesus .. be saved." II Tim. 3:15 - "salvation through faith in Christ." II Thess. 2:3 - "salvation through faith in truth" I Pet. 1:9 - "outcome of your faith … salvation of your souls"	Pelagianism - Choice is basis of one's salvation. Arminianism - Choice of obedience & performance. Evangelicalism - Focus on human action performance. Do this/that

Writing to the Ephesian Christians, Paul explained, "For by grace are you saved through faith…" (Eph. 2:8). In that statement, we see the divine initiative of God's grace connected to the human response of faith in the act of salvation. Grace and faith form a both/and dialectic in Christian thought.

In Jesus Christ "grace appeared bringing salvation to all men" (Titus 2:11), who are "saved through the grace of Jesus" (Acts 15:11). Such saving action of God, however, is "through faith in Christ" (II Tim. 3:15), the receptivity of God's activity in Christ.

There are theological systems that have emphasized God's grace and denied the necessity of possibility of human response. Augustinian/Calvinism is such a system that regards the divine action of grace as solely determinative for human salvation. Pelagianism, on the other hand, focused on the human choice of faith as determinative for individual salvation. Arminianism also focuses on what man does rather than what God does.

Last Things

BOTH ⇌ AND

	Already	Not yet	
Preterism -praeter, past Historicism - God's action in history Postmillennial Triumphalism Diminished expectation of Christ coming again - hope has become realization	Inaugurated eschatology - realized & experienced Jesus is "eschatos man" God's last word for man. I Cor. 15:45 - "last Adam" Finished work of Christ - John 19:30- "it is finished" Christus Victor Acts 2:17 - "in last days, I will pour forth Spirit" Heb. 1:2 - "last days, God has spoken in His Son" I Pet. 1:20 - "appeared in these last times"	Anticipated eschatology - not realized, longed for Jesus is beginning & end of God's work. Second coming of Christ is the consummation and completion of God's redemptive work. Jn. 6:40,44 - "raise him up on last day." I Pet. 1:5 - "salvation revealed in last time." I Jn. 2:18 - "it is last the last hour"	Utopianism Apocalypticism Dispensational Futurism Pessimism - "why polish brass on sinking ship" Projectionism - "pie in the sky bye and bye" Immortality in the future

Christians have long engaged in discussions over differing eschatological opinions of "last things." The scripture record seems to indicate that God's "last in a sequence" activity is both "already" and "not yet" realized.

Jesus is the *"eschatos* Man," the "last Adam" (I Cor. 15:45), who in these "last days" (Acts 2:17; Heb. 1:2) is working out His "finished work" in the lives of Christian people and in His Church. This does not preclude the anticipation of His "second coming" and the "salvation revealed in the last time" (I Pet. 1:5).

To overemphasize the "already" of God's past historical action without anticipation for future consummation diminishes the expectation of Christian hope. On the other hand, inordinate focus on the future return of Jesus Christ can cause Christians to neglect the awareness of all that is available in the "finished work" of Jesus Christ to allow Him to live and work in their present Christian lives.

These dialectic charts will have to suffice in the context of this study, but there are more than 120 additional charts in the aforementioned book, *Two Sides of Every Coin: A Dialectic Formatting of Christian Thought*, which will amplify the both/and dialectic understanding of Christian thought.

We must proceed in this study to consider the next level of our "House of Christian Contrasts." The foundation of the Either/ors and the Framework of the Both/ands we have considered, may have made the reader weary of the theoretical categories of Christian philosophy, theology, and doctrine. Some people enjoy such mental categories of thought, and others "not so much."

Finally, we must all come to the practical question, **"How then shall we live?"**

Only by an
Unfathomable Inclusion
in His life!

There comes a time when every Christian must turn from the theoretical and ideological to the practical and experiential process of living the Christian life. That is where we will now be directing our attention.

When we made the transition from the foundational Either/ors to the framing of Christian thought in the dialectic Both/ands, it required a momentous action on God's part – the "Absolute Paradox" of the incarnation of the Son of God becoming a human person who would live out the character of God as the Perfect Man. We must now consider another momentous occasion between the both/and ideological consideration of dialectic Christian thought and the practical implications of Christian living.

This transition from the "both/ands" to the "seen/unseen" realities of the finishing work of Christian experience may not be as singularly momentous historically as was the incarnation of the Person of Jesus Christ, but it is equally as momentous on a personal experiential level for it entails the individual personification of the birth of Jesus' presence as He is born spiritually in our spirit and lives. The birth of Jesus in Bethlehem was a prototype of His spiritual birth in receptive individuals throughout time. The words of the German mystic poet, John Scheffler, who took the name of Angelus Silesius, explained the connection of these two transitions:

"Though Jesus Christ, a thousand times in Bethlehem be born;
If He's not born in you; your soul is still forlorn."

The historical birth of Christ's incarnation sets up the spiritual "new birth" of Christ in our hearts, and we cannot transition from the dialectic thought-categories to the outliving of the Christ life until the very life of Jesus is birthed and brought into existence in each individual's spirit, who thereby becomes a Christ-one, a Christian, in that process of faithful receptivity.

So, the transition from the framework of the dialectic reciprocity of the both/ands to the top-level finishing works of the Christian life can only come via an **"Unfathomable Inclusion"** of participation in the very life of Jesus Christ. This is a momentous and miraculous reality. Jesus said to Nicodemus, "You must be born again! You must be "born from above" (Jn. 3:3-6), "born not of blood, nor the will of the flesh nor of the will of man, but of God" (Jn. 1:13).

We must go beyond mere assent to the historical and theological tenets of a belief-system, and enter into participation in the very life of the risen and living Lord Jesus in order to experience and re-present His life, the Christ-life, in our Christian lives.

This **"Unfathomable Inclusion"** into participation in the very life of the risen and living Lord Jesus takes us beyond the *objective* thought categories of history and theology, and takes us into the *subjective* experience of receiving the living, experiential Jesus into the core of our spirit. Having received the very life of the living Lord Jesus in spiritual regeneration, the Christian must recognize that the presence of Jesus is not merely a deposit for future benefits, but He desires to "be our life" (cf. Col. 3:4). "For me to live is Christ" (Phil. 1:21), Paul explained. The top level of the "House of Christian Contrasts" explores the implications of how His Life is lived out in our attitudes and behavior.

Unfathomable Inclusion

We are "in Christ"
Christ is "in us"
We are "one spirit with Him"
He lives out HIS life in, through, as us

By the "unfathomable Inclusion," those who are receptive to the living Lord Jesus are **"in Christ."** (We saw this phrase earlier in the either/or section, and it was contrasted with being "in Adam."). "If any man is *in Christ*, he is a new creature; old thing s have passed away, behold all things have become new" (II Cor. 5:17). Our old spiritual identity is cast aside, and "our life is hidden in Christ" (Col. 3:3), with a new spiritual nature, a new spiritual identity as a "Christ-one," a Christian.

We are "in Christ," and **Christ is in us**. In that familiar verse of Gal. 2:20, Paul explains, "I have been crucified with Christ, and it is no longer I who lives, but *Christ lives in me*, and the life I now live in the flesh, I now live by faith in the Son of God who loved me and gave Himself up for me." This is the mystery of the gospel, he explained to the Colossians, "this is the mystery, ... *Christ in you*, the hope of glory" (Col. 1:26,27). Writing to the Corinthians, Paul asked, "Do you not recognize that *Jesus Christ lives in you*, unless you believed in vain?" (II Cor. 13:5).

By the "Unfathomable Inclusion" with the pneumatic Christ, we are "**one spirit with Him.**" We experience a spiritual union with the living Lord Jesus. This is not an essential oneness, whereby as one fellow declared, "I am He, and He is me," for it is usually regarded as blasphemy to claim to BE Jesus. Paul's statement is, "He who is joined to the Lord (Jesus) is *one spirit with Him*" (I Cor. 6:17). Our spiritual union with Christ is a relational union, a participatory union, whereby we are identified by His life in us. We are Christ-ones, Christians.

"Christ is our life," is Paul's way of saying it to the Colossians (Col. 3:4). It is more than just having Christ's spiritual life come to dwell in us as a deposit for heavenly existence. It is more than merely an "eternal life" gift received into the location of our spirit as a deposit for benefits to come in the future. Christ **IS** our life! The only means of identifying who we really are, our deepest identity, is the presence and function of the life of Jesus in and through our lives. The One living the Christian life *in*, *through*, and *as* us is Jesus!

We return to the blueprint, the outline of our "House of Christian Contrasts" study.

We see the foundation of the Either/Ors, the "diametric polarity" of opposites, and the "ultimate incongruity" of how evil could enter the world God created and declared "good." The "Absolute Paradox" of Jesus becoming the God-man in the incarnation, allowed for the Both/And contrasts of the framework of "Dialectic Reciprocity," with the "Indefinite Tension" between equally valid truth-tenets that must not be forced into one-sided, stand-alone positions.

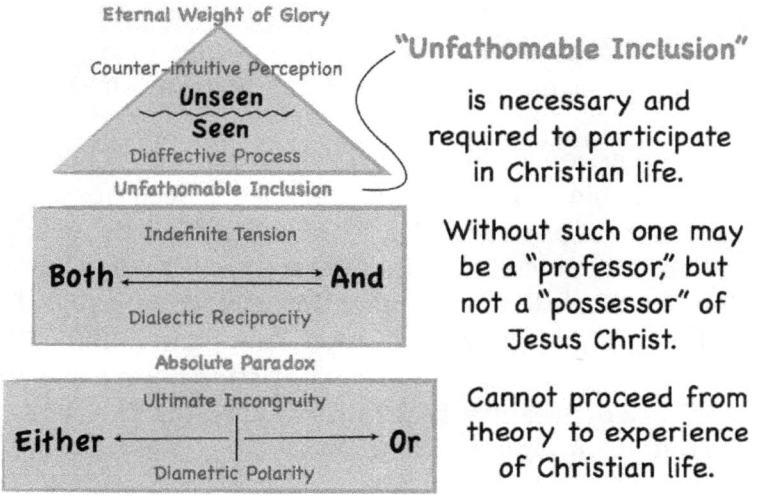

Before we can consider, or experience, the crown and pinnacle of the Christian life, there must be an **"Unfathomable Inclusion"** into the divine life of the Son of God.

This "unfathomable inclusion" **is necessary and required to participate in Christian life**. No one can participate in and live the Christian life unless and until they have received by faith the life of the living Jesus in an "unfathomable inclusion" with Christ.

Without such an "unfathomable inclusion" of spiritual union with the living Christ, one may be a "professor" of Jesus Christ, but not a "possessor" of Jesus Christ. Anyone can make, and many have made a profession of belief in the historicity of Jesus, and even some of the theological implications of the Christ's coming. "Yes, I believe that Jesus was born in Bethlehem, that He died on a cross at Golgotha, even that He was raised from the dead on the third day, and ascended into heaven." I can assent to the Evangelical Statement of Faith which evangelicals consider the criteria of becoming and being a "Christian."

BUT, unless an individual participates in the "unfathomable inclusion" wherein he/she becomes a "possessor" of Jesus Christ, and the Spirit of Christ lives in him/her, and functions as that person's life, they will not enter into what we are representing as a "third level" of the "House of Christian Contrasts." They cannot and will not proceed from mere theory of Christian truth to experience the reality of the Christian life, the Christ-life lived out *in*, *through*, and *as* them.

Christianity is not a believe-right, do right religion! Christianity is **JESUS CHRIST** re-presenting His life in our experience and behavior. Jesus Christ alive and manifesting His life in our mortal bodies (cf. II Cor. 4:10,11).

P.S. – Though reference has been made to being a "possessor" of Jesus Christ, we are referring to the indwelling presence of His life in the Christian. No one can "possess" Jesus Christ in the sense of "owning" Him or "controlling" Him as their possession. The objective is that He "possesses" us, serving as the Lord of our lives. Just thought this clarification needed to be made!

EXPERIENCING THE FINISHING WORK

We must proceed to look at the "Finishing Work," the covering, the roof, the pinnacle, the superstructure of our "House of Christian Contrasts."

The **Foundational** category dealt with the Either/or contrasts of Diametric Polarity, concepts that are antithetical one to the other, disallowing for any middle ground.

The **Framework** stage of our Christian house had to do with the Both/and contrasts of Dialectic Reciprocity, wherein ideas and premises must maintain a tensioned balanced that allows both tenets to be equally valid.

The top tier of our house involves the **Finishing** work of the experiential contrasts of the "seen" and "unseen" perspectives of what is happening in the experiences of our lives.

Just an observation at this point about the interactions of the construction workers in the building of a house.

Some readers may have worked in home construction, perhaps as contractors or specialized construction workers. Some of you have ventured to build your own home. I have had a number of contractor friends who I have been acquainted with through the years. I have observed that between those who deal with foundations, and those who work on the framework of the house, and those who do the finishing work, there is often a bit of friendly contention and chiding. Everyone seems to think that their part of the project is the most important part.

The finishing workers tend to look down their noses at the foundation and frame-workers. "They have no finesse, no attention to detail. They just pour the mud, bang away at the 2x4s, and walk away. They have no sense of aesthetics. What they do is not pretty! The house is totally unlivable. They are just a bunch of 'mud-heads' and 'hammer-goons,' and what they often give us is often not level, not square, not measured precisely. It is the finish workers who make the house a home, make the house livable!" They have to admit, however, that when the foundation and the framing are done properly, it does make the finishing job easier, and the house will be square and solid.

As a corollary, in terms of Christian teachers, there are some who seem to specialize in the "finishing work" of the Christian house. They deal with the experiential factors of the Christian life. They emphasize the spiritual interiority of Christian living, the living out of the Christ-life. They often employ many practical illustrations, and they sometimes look down their noses, and actually diminish the importance of those who teach the foundational theological truths, casting such persons as specializing in sterile doctrine and philosophical ideas.

Conversely, there are times when the foundation-layers and the framers of houses, have a tendency to look down at the finish-workers as wimpy detail-people. "They're just the "pretty-boys! They don't do the heavy-work, the real-man stuff, and they take forever to do what they do. They are just catering to the ladies of the house, making it pretty, and applying all the feel-good stuff."

And in like manner, in the construction of Christian ideas, the foundation-layers and the frame-workers of the house of Christian thought, those who do the in-depth biblical and theological exploration of the either/ors, and look into the dialectic reciprocity of the ideological both/ands; there is sometimes the tendency to project that those who spend the predominant part of their teaching in the experiential and subjective realm of the finishing-touches of the out-living of the Christian life are too preoccupied with the touchy-feely and emotional part of the Christian life. They might be labeled as experientialists, subjectivists, existentialists, behavioralists, or mystics, who deal with the feeling part of the Christian life that cannot really be analyzed, systematized, or proceduralized; they are just the story-tellers, using touching illustrations that tug on people's emotions. The theological analysts have been known to declare that "the important part of the structure is at the bottom, laying out the correct measurements, making it level, making it square, or else it will never stack up correctly."

Yes, things are just as messy among those in Christian house-building, as they are amongst the various contractors of physical house construction. Everyone tends to think that their part is the most important part. In reality, they all have their part and must work together to construct the whole. Paul pointed this out in an agricultural context, explaining that "one plants, one waters, but God gives the growth" (I Cor. 3:7).

There are factors in both the foundation and the framing of a house that will determine how it is finished, whether it be a physical building or a theoretical construction. This is a progressive process from the bottom up, from the ground up.

If we fail to understand the either/or of the Creator/creature, of God/Satan, of God and mankind as foundational to Christian thought; if we fail to understand that the human being is not an independent self, that humans are derivative beings that derive all from God or Satan; then what happens is that people attempt to "finish out" the Christian life by self-effort, the works of their own religious performance. If we do not grasp the dialectic balance of the both/ands, then we fall into the religious ditches of the argumentation of antilectic, i.e. talking against one another, declaring that our doctrines are correct and everyone else's are wrong, with resultant religious conflict.

Looking back at the comprehensive blueprint of our House of Christian Contrasts, we see that we have progressed through the Either/Ors of the Foundation, noted the Absolute Paradox necessary to move from the Either/ors to the Both/and in the God-man, Jesus Christ, and we considered several dialectic charts that demonstrated how Christian thought is framed in Dialectic Reciprocity. We examined the importance of the "Unfathomable Inclusion," that is required and necessary in order to participate in the Christian life, without which we do not have what is necessary to develop the necessary perspective to differentiate between the "seen" and the "unseen" perspectives.

We pointed out that without such an "unfathomable inclusion" whereby the believer is "in Christ," and Christ is in the believer; we are "one spirit with the Spirit of Christ," and the living Lord Jesus actually lives the Christ-life in, through, and as us – without such, one may be a "professor" of Jesus Christ (professing that they believe the Either/ors and the Both/ands of Christian thought), but without the "unfathomable inclusion" the individual is not a "possessor" of Jesus Christ, and allowing the Lord Jesus Christ to possess their whole being.

Such an individual is unable to proceed from the theory of the Christian life to the actual and practical experience of the Christian life in the top-tier of our "House of Christian Contrasts." Without "participation in Christ" via the "unfathomable spiritual inclusion," the top story cannot be constructed on the house of Christian thought.

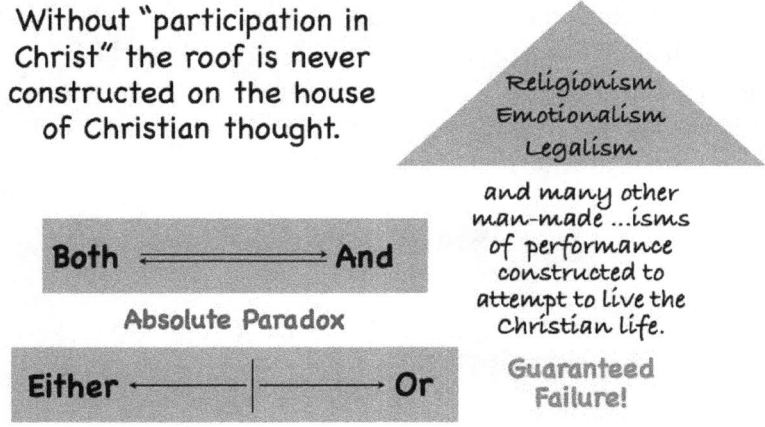

What has happened is that religion has often attempted to put a roof on the house that is not God's intent. It ends up being a cobbled-up loft of religionism, emotionalism, legalism, and many other man-made -isms of human performance constructed in an attempt to live the Christian life.

What does this produce? **Guaranteed failure**! The Christian House becomes merely a believe-right, do-right religious construct, and many individual Christians never really participate in the "experiential finishing process," – the apex, the pinnacle of the Christian life.

This top level of the "House of Christian Contrasts" is different from the previous two. It is the capstone, the finishing process of the gospel. This is where we have to get out of the mental boxes and into the crucible of Christian living. We move from the analytical to the experiential, from thought-processes to life-processes, from reasoned thought to practical living. Logical and cerebral ideologues often have a difficult time in this third tier. Rationalists tend to pull their hair out trying to figure it out. The pragmatism of the natural world considers it absurd or irrational. Some philosophers call it "existential," as was the tag applied to the thought of the Danish thinker, Soren Kierkegaard.

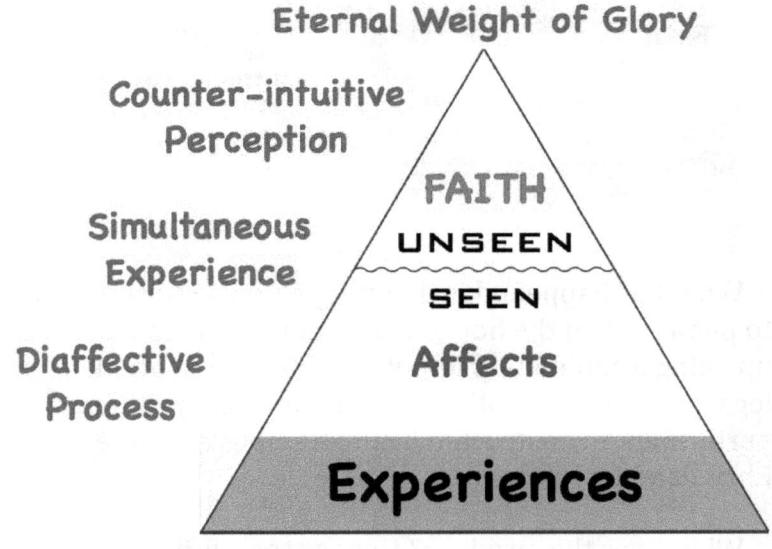

In this third level of the Christian house, we must begin by recognizing that every person must face and deal with the "**Experiences**" of life. Christians have not been given an "exemption" from experiencing and suffering all of the experiences that human beings in general experience. The Christian life is not "Easy Street." It is not an escape from the hardships of life.

The question is: How does a Christian deal with the difficult experiences of life? How do we allow those experiences to "**affect**" our mental attitudes, emotions, and decisions? Do we allow our natural **affects** to cause us to **react** to these circumstantial experiences in the same ways that the world around us reacts? No doubt, we often DO! But, we must explore how Christians can draw upon the indwelling resource of the Spirit of Christ in **FAITH** that allows for the receptivity of His divine activity?

"SEEN" Perspective

natural, temporal – visceral, visual

Surface level –

how experiences AFFECT us

How we REACT to those experiences

... happy?   ... stressed?
... rejected?   ... seek religion?

Diaffective Process

The "seen" perspective of our natural reactions can be overridden by the "unseen" perspective of recognizing how God in Christ by the Spirit desires to manifest His character in our lives.

In this top-tier of the Christian House of Contrasts all Christians, undoubtedly and inevitably, have the **simultaneous experience** of both the natural "seen" reactions, as well as the supernatural "unseen" response of FAITH.

In what we are calling the **"Diaffective Process,"** we want to understand how we can *move through* the natural reactionary "affects" to that **counter-intuitive perspective** whereby we experientially participate in the "ways of God" by faith, and allow "the eternal weight of glory" to be evidenced in our lives here and now.

"UNSEEN" Perspective

eternal, supernatural – spiritual

**Taking the time to RESPOND
to the experiences of life
with the choice of FAITH
– our receptivity of His activity.**

Counterintuitive perspective

The text that we are using to inspire our thinking in this "seen" and "unseen" category is from Paul's words in II Corinthians 4:7-19.

> "**7** But we have this treasure in earthen vessels, so that the surpassing greatness of the power will be of God and not from ourselves; **8** *we are* afflicted in every way, but not crushed; perplexed, but not despairing; **9** persecuted, but not forsaken; struck down, but not destroyed; **10** always carrying about in the body the dying of Jesus, so that the life of Jesus also may be manifested in our body. **11** For we who live are constantly being delivered over to death for Jesus' sake, so that the life of Jesus also may be manifested in our mortal flesh. **12** So death works in us, but life in you.
> **13** But having the same spirit of faith, according to what is written, "I believed, therefore I spoke," we also believe, therefore we also speak, **14** knowing that He who raised the Lord Jesus will raise us also with Jesus and will present us with you. **15** For all things *are* for your sakes, so that the grace which is spreading to more and more people may cause the giving of thanks to abound to the glory of God.
> **16** Therefore we do not lose heart, but though our outer man is decaying, yet our inner man is being renewed day by day. **17** For momentary, light affliction is producing for us an **eternal weight of glory** far beyond all comparison, **18** while we look not at the things which are **seen**, but at the things which are **not seen**; for the things which are seen are **temporal**, but the things which are not seen are **eternal**."

It is necessary to point out that our objective in this top-story of the Christian House of Contrasts is to participate in a "**Counter-intuitive Perspective**." To allow the Christ-life to be lived out in us will be counter-intuitive to the natural way of seeing things and doing things. It will be counter-cultural, for the natural world culture is certainly contrary to Christ's character. And it will be counter-productive, because the pragmatism of the world, especially American society, considers *quantitative productivity* as the ultimate goal, whereas the *qualitative objective of character* is the way of Christ. God's ways are not the world's way, in fact they are 180 degrees opposite (cf. Isa. 55:8,9) of the perspective of the world.

In Christ's way of living, everything is counter-intuitive, as these statements reveal:

The way up is down. The world says, "the way up is to climb the ladder to the top rung." The Christian perspective advocates the "humility that considers another better than oneself" (Phi. 2:3).

The way to be exalted is to be humbled. Jesus, for example, "humbled Himself, even unto death, and God highly exalted Him" (Phil. 2:8,9). "Humble yourselves before the Lord, and He will exalt you" (James 4:10).

The way to gain is to lose. Jesus said, "what does it profit a man to gain the whole world and forfeit his soul? Whoever loses His life for My sake and the gospel will gain it (and be saved)" (Mk. 8:26).

The way to increase is to decrease. In the words of John the Baptist concerning Jesus: "He must increase; I must decrease" (Jn. 3:30).

The way to be rich is to be poor. In the beatitudes, Jesus said, "Blessed are the poor in spirit, for they will inherit the kingdom" (Matt. 5:3).

The way to invest is to divest. Jesus told the rich young ruler, "Get rid of what you are hanging on to, and give it to the poor" (Matt. 19:21).

The way to experience joy is to suffer. I Peter 4:12 - "to the degree you share the sufferings of Christ, keep on rejoicing."

The way to be strong is to be weak. Paul writes in II Cor. 12:10 - "when I am weak, then I am strong" (in His strength). "The weakness of God is stronger than men" (I Cor. 1:25).

The way to be wise is to be foolish. I Cor. 3:18,19 - "if a man thinks he is wise, he must become foolish." Human knowledge will not suffice. "The foolishness of God is wiser than men" (I Cor. 1:25).

The way to live is to die. Identification with Christ's death is the way to fullness of life in Christ Jesus. Some call it the "cross-life." "I have been crucified with Christ; it is no longer I who live, but Christ lives in me" (Gal. 2:20).

The way to enlarge is to reduce. We get rid of the peripherals and superficialities of life is to enlarge our relationship with Christ.

The way to be useful is to be useless. Jesus told the "parable of the useless servant" (Lk. 17:7-10), who recognized that his usefulness was in his uselessness.

The way to be powerful is to be powerless. We recognize our powerlessness in order to allow His divine power to be implemented.

The way to move forward is to wait. Those who wait for the Lord will gain new strength; They will mount up *with* wings like eagles; They will run and not get tired; They will walk and not become weary (Isa. 40:31).

The way to win is to admit defeat. We overcome when we come to the conclusion, "I can't; only HE can!"

The way to succeed is to fail. It is in our failures that we learn what does not work, and we turn to the One who does all things well.

The way to overcome is to turn the other cheek. "Do not resist, but turn the other cheek" (Matt. 5:39).

The way to work is to rest. As we rest in His sufficiency, His divine works will be expressed in our lives.

The way to get is to give. "Give, and it will be given to you" (Luke 6:38).

The way to rule is to serve. Jesus, the Ruler of the Universe, served His disciples by washing their feet (Jn. 13:5-8). He told His disciples, "He who would be first, must become servant of all" (Mk. 9:35).

The way to be first is to be last. "The last shall be first, and the first, last" (Matt. 20:16).

The way to conquer is to love. "We are more than conquerors through Christ who loved us" (Rom. 8:37).

The way to heaven is through hell. "Heaven can be entered only through the narrow gate" (Matt. 7:13), and that involves difficulty.

The way to commit is to submit. We "submit ourselves to God" (James 4:7) for all that He is committed to be and do in us.

The world system will never understand the premises and promises on which the Christian functions, because they are backwards and illogical to the humanistic mode of operation – counter-intuitive!

The experiences of life are inevitable. We are alive on planet earth, and human life on planet earth is comprised of experiences, events, situations, circumstances, etc. We want to consider how those experiences *affect* us, and whether we can "move through" the natural affects in the "**seen**" perspective to an "**unseen**" perspective that the world of natural mankind knows nothing about. The natural affectations and reactions to what is occurring in the daily lives of Christians while living in this world can be overcome by the supernatural provision of the activity of God's grace in the living Lord Jesus as we respond in faithful receptivity of God's character.

The Experiences of Life

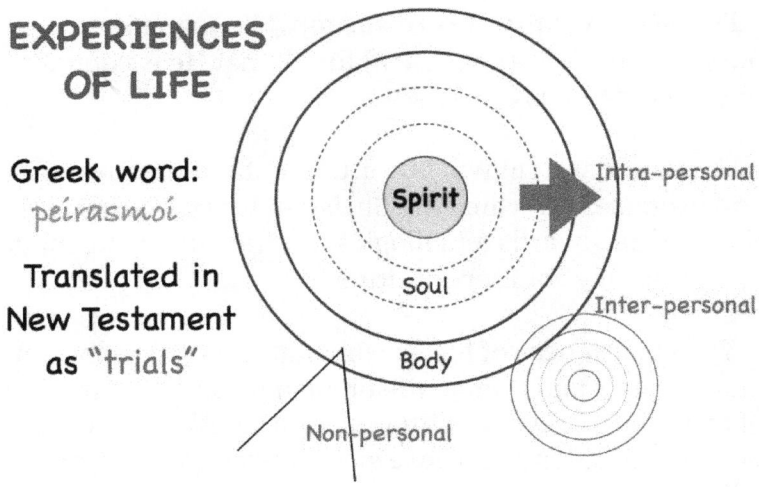

We begin by noting the obvious, that "stuff happens" in all of our lives, and it is often not a pleasant experience. The "negatives of life" inevitably occur. The world refers to this phenomenon as "Murphy's law" – "if anything can go wrong it will." Perhaps you have heard of "O'Malley's comment on Murphy's Law" – "Murphy was an optimist." Within the experiences of life in this world, unexpected circumstances happen time and time again. We don't have to try to create this "stuff," or go looking for a problem. It just happens! The Christian response to such is to accept these "seen" circumstances as a prelude and introduction to what God wants to do in our lives, believing that "God is working all things for good" (Rom. 8:28) in our lives.

Many Christians have the misconception that life should be free of problems. Is that not the "rest" that Jesus promised (Matt. 11:28), a life free of problems? NO!

Life is messy! Life is precarious. Life is NOT fair, and God never promised that it would be! Don't let anyone tell you otherwise. If you've been advised otherwise, you've been sold a "false bill of goods." Some preachers have said: "If you're having troubles, you are outside of God's will, you just don't have enough faith." That is not true!

II Cor. 2: 17 – "We are not like those hucksters—and there are many of them—whose idea in getting out the Gospel is to make a good living out of it." There are hucksters, hawkers, peddlers, who sugar-coat the gospel, and want to sell you a false bill of goods. The gospel is not a utopian message. It is not an "all is well" message! It is not a "this will pay off" message.

Life is messy. It is not clear-cut, slick, "smooth sailing on the seas of life;" it is not membership in God's "red-carpet club." There is no such thing as a "Teflon Christian life," where stuff doesn't stick, and there are no sharp edges!

We are all involved in messy Christian life. Michael Yaconelli published a book entitled, *Messy Spirituality*. We all have messy family situations. Let us not kid ourselves, and play games of "cover-up" with others. Some Christians do not want to be honest about their lives. They want to protect God's reputation and convey that they are living a "victorious Christian life." Too often, it is just a charade, and when it all caves in their lack of truth-telling is revealed. Then people say, "See, just like I thought – that Christianity stuff doesn't work; it's just a spiritual sugar pill."

Life will always be messy here on planet earth. This is where we all live – all of us! We don't want to deceive ourselves, and live in denial, and pretend that we have entered into some kind of triumphalism or victory where we don't get dirty, don't get stuck anymore, and we have no failures.

Have you noticed the abundance of words we have developed for the trials and experiences of life? Ex. problems, troubles, hardships, offences, scandals, suffering, adversity, failures, tragedy, pressures, tribulation, sickness, illness, "aches and pains," accidents, persecution, unpleasant situations., catastrophes, disasters, disciplines, stress, persecution, and the list goes on! Eliphaz told Job, "Man is born for trouble" (Job 5:7).

There is always something going wrong. Ex. automobile, house, appliances, relationships (especially family), husband and wife; parent/children; finances, religious involvement. The status-quo of our lives is always, relentlessly, being punctured with problems. The circumstances of life on planet earth will inevitably involve adversity. The problems of life often cause Christians perplexity (II Cor. 4:8), distress (Lk. 12:50), confusion, grief, and these are not necessary wrong.

I Pet. 4:12 – "Beloved, do not be surprised at the fiery ordeal which comes upon you for your testing, as though some strange thing were happening to you." "It must needs be that offenses come" – Matt 18:7; Lk. 17:1 (Greek *scandalan* from which we get English "scandals"). Other translations read "temptations, stumbling blocks."

Tribulation is part of our everyday lives. "Tribulation" comes from the Latin word *tribulum* = pressure. "John 16:33 - "in this world you have tribulation." Acts 14:22 – Paul and Barnabas, "through many tribulations we must enter the kingdom of God." Rom. 5:3 – "we exult in our tribulations, knowing that tribulation brings about endurance." Romans 12:12 – we persevere in tribulation."

There will always be tough times and opposition. **WHY**? It's inexplicable. That's the way life is! Sometimes, we think that we have more than our share. Sometimes, we feel like we are "under the pile." We may be "under water" financially. We may feel like we are "under appreciated." Sometimes these situations are never resolved. Sometimes the situation looms so large and threatening that we don't know if there's any way out of the pain. People seek to escape, even commit suicide.

WHY does God allow this "stuff"? "His ways are past finding out" (Rom. 11:33). "God's ways are not our ways" (Isa. 55:8,9). Some have called it "the enigma of the Christian life." Or the "anomaly of Christianity." God has a way of throwing "curve balls." "Where did that come from?" Prov. 20:24 – "Since the Lord is directing our steps, why try to understand everything that happens along the way."

Christians, along with the world, may blame their circumstances on "bad luck," but since they usually have some awareness of the spiritual world, they often blame their problems either on the devil or on God. "The devil's after me; he caused my problem today (flat tire, tripped on sidewalk, etc.). They give too much credit to the devil.

Other Christians might say, "God has done this to me!" "God is sovereign, and in charge of everything, so He must have caused this tragedy in my life." "He is the one who gave, or at least allowed, my mother to have cancer, or my daughter to have a car wreck." "What have I done wrong for God to do this to me?" "God must be punishing me!" Such Christians often do not understand the character of God in Christ. God is FOR us, not against us! He always loves us, God is LOVE (I Jn. 4:8,16). God is not a punitive God!

God is the essential cause of all things because He is the Creator God from whence all things come into being, but He is not the blameworthy or culpable cause of evil that is contrary to His character of absolute good.

Greek word: peirasmoi

Trials, Testings, or Temptations

I Cor. 10:13

"No trial/testing/temptation has overtaken you
but such as is common to man;
and God is faithful, who will not allow you to be
tried/tested/tempted beyond what you are able,
but with the trial/testing/temptation will
provide the way of escape also,
so that you will be able to endure it."

In the New Testament, the word for "trials" is *peirasmoi*. It is derived from root word *peiro*, meaning "to pierce." Trials are the situations of life which tend to pierce our status-quo, what we have planned to make our lives stable and comfortable. These situations test and examine our mind-set and responses, to see whether we will react with self-sufficiency or respond with faith in God. By the way, *peirasmoi* in modern Greek usage, is translated "experiences."

None of us are immune or exempt from the situations, circumstances, and experiences that occur in this world. God does not give Christians a "pass" from any of the *peirasmoi* trials of this world. Christians are often trying to figure out "why" God allowed this trial. Does God want to make me stronger, better, more spiritual, to develop character in me, to perfect me, to make me mature? Perhaps, I am like a diamond in the rough and God is chipping away, shaping and polishing me to make me sparkle. They tell me that Viking ships were made from trees that survived the severe storms of Norway. Is God allowing me to go through the storms of life so I will be a strong Christian? What is God trying to teach me? Is God just giving me the privilege of "suffering for Jesus," so I can better identify with Him? Is God preparing me for ministry?

Too many Christians are filled with self-concern; they are attempting to evaluate life from the perspective, "It's all about ME." The Christian life is not about ME; it is always about HIM. God wants to manifest and re-present the life of Jesus in our mortal bodies and behavior.

It will be instructive to consider how the trials and experiences of life come in several forms:

(1) Non-personal trials.

These experiences may be as minor as a pesky mosquito, a stubbed toe, or a squeaky door. On the other hand, they may involve major adversity and tragedy. These non-personal trials may be unpleasant, ex. flat tire, engine in your automobile blows up, house burns down, wrench slips, catch the flu, an appliance in the kitchen will not work. They can be pleasant, ex. found a hundred-dollar bill on the sidewalk, child graduates from high school or college, stock market goes up. Job 1:21 – "the Lord gives and the Lord takes away." Paul's "thorn in the flesh" (II Cor. 12) seems to have been a non-personal trial.

Some of the non-personal experiences we must confront are much bigger – the situations in the world around us – politics, economics, weather, social phenomena, etc., and some people get all agitated in their reaction to these situations also. We all have big and small non-personal experiences, from presidential politics to an individual hangnail.

(2) Interpersonal trials.

These are the experiences that involve interaction with other people. They are inevitable. "No man is an island," and we all have interpersonal relationships. If we are married there are the trials between husband and wife. If we have children we encounter the parent/child situations (and these do not usually end when they leave home). It may be experiences with our neighbors. If we are in a working situation, it may be the boss or other employees. It may be a social group or club you participate in, a "booster-club" for an activity your children are involved in. Other people have differing personalities, they think and feel differently, they act and react differently. These situations may produce unpleasant experiences. They may get on our nerves, rub us the wrong way, create interpersonal friction. Some people are just plain weird and stupid! There can also be pleasant interpersonal experiences, the boss nominates you for a promotion, or a raise. Some biblical examples of interpersonal situations: Gn. 35-50 – Joseph was sold into slavery by his jealous brothers. Was it fair? NO. Did God use it for good? YES! Jesus was falsely charged and convicted in a kangaroo court. Fair? NO. Did God use it for good? YES.

(2) Intrapersonal trials.

These are situations and experiences that come from within us. They are rooted within our psyche, within the desires of our soul. They may stem from addictive patterns that have developed in the desires that run through our minds, emotions and wills. In trying to explain these, people might blame such on "the dirty old man that lives in me," or my depraved sinful human nature, or that "I just seem to have a 'dirty mind'." Have you ever been sitting in a church service and your mind starts thinking of and focusing on something that doesn't seem to have anything to do with the things of God? It might be a task you have to do. It might be an inner desire to sin. It might even be something sexual, perhaps a vile thought. "WHY am I thinking about that in the middle of the church worship service?"

There is a cosmic spiritual conflict going on between God and Satan, between good and evil. On the larger social scale, the battleground may be our culture or civilization. On an individual basis, our soul is often the battleground of the spiritual forces. Christians need to be aware that spiritual solicitations will occur from both God and Satan in the midst of our trials and experiences

This is where the New Testament language gets a little muddy and muddled. The Greek was a very precise language, but there are words that have multiple meanings and connotations. One of those words is the Greek word *peirasmoi* that we mentioned earlier. We saw that it meant "trial," the situations or circumstances of life, with the modern usage "experiences." But the verb form of the same word is *peirazo*, and refers to the solicitations of the spiritual powers that are employed in the midst of our experiences. So, in the midst of our *peirasmoi* (our trials and experiences), we are *peirazoed* (solicited to react or respond) by the spirit-beings of both God and Satan, and the same verb is used for both! This can be confusing!

Temptation

The one who tempts is the tempter.

Temptation to ACT	Temptation to REACT
• Personal Aspiration	• Fight
• Personal Gratification	• Fright
• Personal Reputation	• Flight

The spirit-forces – God or Satan – in the midst of every circumstance in our lives are soliciting us to draw from and depend on their character in the midst of the situation. When Satan, the tempter, seduces and assails and entices us, we refer to his action of *peirazoing* us in the midst of our *peirasmoi* experiences as "tempting" us. Paul wrote to the Thessalonians (I Thess. 3:5)- "I sent to find out about your faith, for fear that the tempter (*peirazon*) might have tempted (*peirazoed*) you." When the Greek word has a negative connotation of soliciting a person with evil intent, then we translate the verb as "to tempt," and the noun form as "temptation."

But if the same verb *peirazo* is used of God's action, entreating and soliciting us to respond with His character, then we translate the verb "to test" and the noun form as "tests." Heb. 11:17 indicates that "God tested (*peirazoed*) Abraham" when He led him to the mountain to see if he would sacrifice his son in obedience to God. Jesus asked Philip where they were going to find bread to feed the 5000 people on the far side of the Sea of Galilee, and He did so in order to "test" (*peirazo*) him (Jn. 6:5,6). When God engages in such action, He is not trying to trip us up or cause us to stumble, but He examines our hearts to see if we will respond in FAITH that recognizes His sufficiency to manifest His character. That is always what God desires, to manifest His character in His creation unto His own glory.

Satan, on the other hand, solicits us to manifest his character of selfishness and sinfulness in the midst of our experiences in life. And in every situation, we will manifest one character or the other, sinfulness or godliness, derived from one spiritual source or the other. "Whatever is not of faith is sin" (Rom. 14:23), but the Christian has "Christ in you, the hope of glory" (Col. 1:27), in order to manifest the glorious character of God to the glory of God. As Jesus said, "Apart from Me you can do nothing" (Jn. 15:5) that is godly.

What we are describing is not an equal dualistic battle, however, for "greater is He who is in you, than he who is in the world" (I Jn. 4:4).

In I Cor. 10:13 the difficulty of translating the word *peirasmoi* is evident. Is Paul saying, "No *temptation* has overtaken you, but such as is common to man?" Or is he saying, "No *trial* has overtaken you, but such as is common to man?" Or is he saying, "No *testing* has overtaken you, but such as is common to man?" Different English translations use all three of those words.

The trials, the tempting, and the testing, they all happen simultaneously. In the midst of a *trial*/experience, we will be *tempted* by the tempter, Satan, to act and react with his character; but the entire situation will also be a *testing* of the Lord to see whether we recognize His sufficiency in the situation, and are willing to respond in faith, our receptivity of His activity that allows His character to be manifested to His glory.

We are all tempted, and we all succumb to temptation. We previously mentioned that the noun *peirasmoi* can refer to the solicitations of the tempter suggesting that we act and react with his character of selfishness and sinfulness. It is important to note that the source of temptation is not from God. God is involved in our "testing," in order to provide opportunities for faith, but not in tempting us to evil character. "Let no one say when he is tempted, 'I am being tempted by God;' for God cannot be tempted by evil, and He Himself does not tempt anyone" (James 1:13).

Neither are we tempted by the world around us, even though it is a fallen world; the world is simply the context of the trials and temptation. Neither are we tempted by the "flesh" patterns of sinfulness and selfishness that are in the desires of our soul. We all have our unique patterns that have developed in the desires of our soul. But they do not tempt us, despite the misunderstanding of James 1:14,15.

The source of the solicitation of temptation is always the tempter – Satan, the devil, the deceiver, the accuser of the brethren. Matt. 4:1 – Jesus was led by the Spirit into the wilderness to be tempted (*peirazoed*) by the *tempter* (the *peirazon*). I Cor. 7:5 – "Husbands and wives should not deprive one another, but should come together so that *Satan* will not tempt (*peirazo*) you." I Thess. 3:5 – Paul writes to the Thessalonians "for fear that the *tempter* (*peiron*) might have tempted (*peirazoed*) you." The tempter is always the subject of the verb "to tempt."

God purposed that human beings should be tempted. He meant for us to use our "freedom of choice," to have a true genuine option. It's not a real choice unless the antithesis is a viable option. But Satan's purpose is to seduce us to act or react with his selfish character in such a way that we might misrepresent who we are in Christ, to live in alleged self-sufficiency whereby we try to act with self-effort of performance, engaging in the lie of self-improvement, trying to operate as an "independent self" in order "to be all we can be." The Devil works particularly as the "accuser of the brethren" (Rev. 12:10), of Christians. "So, you claim to be a 'new creature in Christ...' (II Cor. 5:17)? He can certainly quote scripture. So, "Christ lives in you" (Gal. 2:20; Col. 1:27; II Cor. 13:5? How's that going? "You say you're righteous, holy, perfect in Christ...? "You don't seem to look righteous, holy and perfect all the time. Your behavior is inconsistent, you know. Do you feel righteous, holy and perfect all the time? You know that how you feel, and what you do, is the basis of who you really are, your real identity," he disingenuously lies to us. Those are the kinds of LIES that Satan accuses Christian with. If you have read C.S. Lewis' *Screwtape Letters* you are aware that the tempter even tempts Christians to be more "religious," more dedicated, more committed, more "spiritual," because he knows that such self-effort leads either to condemnation, defeat and guilt feelings, or to "spiritual pride" in some form of perfectionism where we think we've "arrived" in our Christian walk by our self-effort, so that we pat ourselves on the back, saying, "What a good girl am I."

It is important for Christians to be aware of how the tempter works. II Cor. 2:11 – "in order that no advantage be taken of us by Satan; for we are not ignorant of his schemes."

Satan tempts us both to **ACT** and **REACT**.

ACT – I John 2:16 – "all that is in the world, the lust of the flesh and the lust of the eyes and the boastful pride of life, is NOT from the Father, but is from the world," from the diabolic "ruler of this world" (Jn. 12:31; 16:11). The "lust of the eyes" may refer to "personal aspiration," the desire to possess for myself. The "lust of the flesh" may refer to "personal gratification," the desire to please myself. The "boastful pride of life" may refer to "personal reputation," the desire to promote myself. Those seem to sum up Satan's selfishness, his personal-interest agenda, whereby we think we can exclaim, "I did it MY way!"

REACT – Satan also motivates a self-oriented prompting to REACT to the situations of life, to the non-personal and interpersonal trials. When we think our self-interests have been thwarted by an event or by another person, we are tempted to react with:

Fight – anger, hostility, rage, retaliation, resentment, bitterness, blame, judgmentalism. Someone gets promoted and you did not. "It's not fair!"

Fright – fear, anxiety, worry. You do not get invited to the women's bible study. "They don't like me; what's wrong with me?"

Flight – escape, evasion, withdrawal, conflict avoidance, ambivalence, indifference, cynicism, apathy…. "Well, if people won't be fair to me, and don't like me, then I'm not going to stick around and get kicked around. I'll just quit and go to another church."

It is very important to explain that temptation is NOT sin! I recall hearing a radio preacher declare, "If you are being tempted, you are outside of the will of God. You do not have enough faith." **FALSE!** If you are being tempted by the tempter, it just means that you are still alive on planet earth. They have not yet put you in a wooden box, and lowered it into the ground.

Temptation in our thought-life has led some Christians to reason, "Well, I thought the thought, I might as well do the act." **NO!** "But, if I really loved God, I wouldn't have that thought." **NO!** Temptation comes to our mind and emotions as a suggestion, as a solicitation of Satan to act and react with character contrary to the character of God, i.e. in a sinful manner. Satan, the tempter, is the "accuser of the brethren" (Rev. 12:10).

Sin, the manifestation of character contrary to the character of God, occurs only in the freely chosen response of a human being to the temptation, in the freely chosen decision of the will to accept Satan's solicitation/invitation, to connect with and be receptive to Satan's suggestion of selfish behavior. Sin is not in the temptation or solicitation of the tempter, but becomes evident when we choose to allow the Evil One to become operative in us to manifest his selfish and sinful character.

It is not that Christians should desire to be without any temptation or solicitation to selfish character and behavior, but that we should be aware of and wise to the schemes and wiles of the devil (cf. II Cor. 2:11; I Pet. 5:8). Henry Drummond once wrote, "The greatest of all temptations is to want to be without any." Christians need to recognize that it is in the opposing instigation toward sinful selfishness that we exercise our freedom of choice, and function as choosing creatures in the midst of the circumstances of life.

It is not necessarily wrong to want to be delivered from the weight of our problems, the pile of situations that we are confronted with. Everyone wants to find a way to deal with the situations, but the self-centered humanistic "how-tos" that the world suggests do not work!

It should also be noted that indecision can also be a decision. "I don't want to have to deal with it, so I'll just avoid it, put it off, close my eyes and hope that it goes away." The avoidance of making a decision concerning what is occurring in the situations of life is a decision that may prolong or intensify the problem at hand.

AFFECTIVITY

Our choices in the midst of life's situations reveal how we have allowed the circumstances, as well as the tempting solicitations of the Tempter, to "affect" us. Everyone is affected by what is happening in their lives, but our reactive "affects" can exacerbate the problem, or calm the situation in order to navigate through the problem. It is often our reactive "affects," our selfish concerns, thoughts and emotions in response to the situation, that cause more problem than the circumstance itself.

The psychological community refers quite often to the "negative affectivity" whereby some people react to the situations of life, allowing the circumstances to "affect" them negatively. They admit that "negative affectivity" is a code name for "neuroticism," but will not admit that it is quite synonymous with a selfish and sinful reactive choice to what people encounter in life.

British missionary, Norman Grubb, explained, "Our troubles are never happenings in themselves, but the **affect** we allow them to have upon us." This is quite consistent with what others have said. Epictetus – "Men are disturbed not by things, but by the views which they take of them." Montaigne – "A man is hurt not so much by what happen, as by his opinion of what happens." Wade Boggs – Our lives are not determined by what happens to us, but how we react to what happens." G.K Chesterton – "An inconvenience is only an adventure wrongly considered. An adventure is an inconvenience rightly considered."

The experiences of life are inevitable. Trials and tribulations (*peirasmoi*) are just part of life. In the midst of such situations our personal affectivity is inevitable, as we act and react to what is happening around and within us.

Our objective in considering the "experiences" of life and our personal reactive "affects" in the midst of such occurrences is to explain that Christians have the divine resource to "move through" the natural and normal "affects" that humans have to the experiences of life, via the "*Diaffective* Process," simultaneously experiencing both the temporal and "seen," but moving into the counterintuitive perspective of the "unseen" and eternal where we experience God at work in our lives. There we can fulfill the purpose of our existence by allowing the "eternal glory" of God to be seen in our behavior.

There is no doubt that the world views Christian behavior as an escapist endeavor; a mental escape into the ethereal that tries to gloss over the painful realities of life here on earth. The world seems to think that Christians are running into their mental cave of "spirituality," and then touting, "God causes all things to work together for good" (Rom. 8:28). That, of course, does not begin to be what the Christian life is about. Christians should be very realistic about living in the world, and about the experiences of life in this world. We are "in the world, but not of the world" (Jn. 17:11,14).

Our reactions are closely watched by the world around us, and they do reveal how the experiences of life "affect" us. A common natural reaction is to ask WHY? Why has this happened to me? WHY Lord? As if God were required to explain Himself for everything in our lives.

THE SEEN PERSPECTIVE

The "seen" perspective is the realm of the natural reactions of self- concern, self-interest, and self-consciousness. Steve Pettit once said that self-consciousness was at the heart of all Christians' sins. I had to ponder and process that statement, but soon realized how Christians are so conscious of themselves. "How am I doing in this Christian life?" "Am I doing it correctly?" "Am I being the Christian, God wants me to be?" But, it's not about US; it's about HIM. The Christian life is about **JESUS**. That is why it is called the CHRIST-Life. It's not for us to keep taking our "spiritual temperature."

We have such a tendency to be concerned about ourselves. The "seen" perspective is where we react in our typical, natural way, thinking that we are an "independent self" that has to figure this out and "pull it off" in a way that looks "Christian" and pleases God. We operate with the fallen premise that "I am my own center of reference."

When we act and react in the "seen" perspective, we are usually reacting in accord with the "flesh" patterns of selfish and sinful orientation that are the residual ruts of Satan's character in the desires of our soul. We are acting and reacting with the personal interest agenda of the Evil One.

The spiritual reality that Christians need to understand is that we are "new creatures" in Christ. We have a new spiritual identity. We are no longer "sinners," but "saints;" yes, "holy ones," "righteous ones," "perfect ones," not inherently, but derived from the Holy One, the

Righteous One, the Perfect One, JESUS CHRIST, who resides in our spirit. We are the sons and daughters of God. We are Christ-ones, Christians, because Jesus has become our life, His Spirit in our spirit. That should be our Christian focus – the living Lord Jesus, and who we are "in Him."

Col. 1:27 - "this is the mystery, Christ in you the hope of glory."

Gal. 2:20 - "I have been crucified with Christ; it is no longer I who lives, but Christ lives in me."

II Cor. 13:5 - "do you not recognize that Jesus Christ is in you, unless you believed in vain."

The Christian still has the "flesh patternings," and there is a behavioral conflict going on in the Christian life; "the flesh sets its desire against the Spirit" (Gal. 5:17). Some Christians seem to have been developed the mistaken idea that being a Christian is "smooth-sailing on the seas of life," a "rest" from all difficulties, or moving into "fantasyland" at Disneyland. Some complain that it is more difficult to deal with life after they became a Christian than before. That makes sense, for the unregenerate are "slaves of sin" (Rom. 6:6), and they just "go with the flow" of Satan's character, following their own desires, in the pattern of selfish pleasure that Epicurus taught. Some Christians have even complained, "Jesus makes life miserable!"

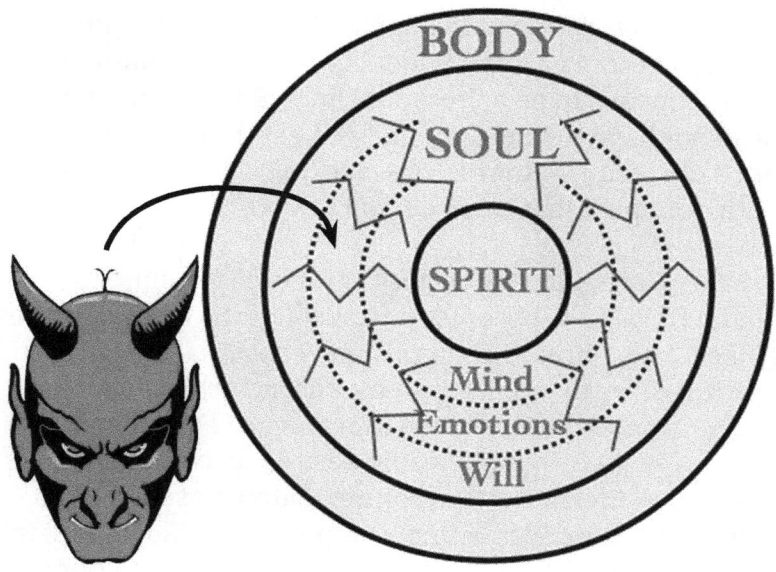

Christians still have the old flesh-patterns, and that is made all the more difficult as the tempter, Satan, the one who was sent into exile when we were regenerated, fires his "fiery darts" (Eph. 6:16) into our lives and goes fishing under the very desires he helped to form (cf. James 1:14). He knows right where to lure and entice us. The devil knows the buttons of our susceptibility, vulnerability and weakness; just where to "get under our skin" and solicit us to "plug into" his character to re-enact the old action and reaction patterns. Remember, it is always the tempter who tempts us. It is NOT the flesh-patterns of our desires, for they have no substantive, animate, personification by which to solicit us to exhibit character.

We must look a little closer at the behavioral and experiential conflict that occurs in the Christian life. The

Christian has received the Spirit of Christ in the human spirit to become a Christ-one. That is the bottom-line of what it means to be a Christian. Rom. 8:9 - "if anyone does not have the Spirit of Christ, he is none of His (i.e. not a Christian)." Rom. 8:16 - "the Spirit bears witness with our spirit that we are a son of God."

Every Christian recognizes that there is an inner conflict. We have become "partakers of the divine nature" (II Pet. 1:4), Christ-ones with a new spiritual identity. The Spirit desires to manifest divine character through our God-given desires, but the patternings of selfish and sinful character in our "fleshly desires" provide the residual platform for the tempter, Satan, to solicit us to consent and connect with his empowering and energizing to manifest his character via those patternings in our desires. Oh, so crafty, he suggests that this is our standard, time-tested *modus operandi* for acting and reacting. This the way we know best. We know how to deal with the outcomes of these choices and reactions. And so, we are solicited to misrepresent who we are in Christ, and behave contrary to who we have become!

Sometimes it feels like we have an experiential schizophrenia, whereby we are being pulled in two different directions. We must remember, though, that this is NOT a spiritual schizophrenia, like those who suggest that we have "two natures" in our spirit, or that we have two simultaneous identities, or that we are only half-righteous or half-holy, only half regenerated in spiritual condition. The conflict that Paul mentions between the Spirit and the "flesh" is primarily on the experiential, subjective "feeling" level in our soul.

It is not a spirit-issue. That has been settled. The Spirit of Christ dwells in our spirit. The conflict is a battle between two spirits, the spirit of the Evil One and the Spirit of God in Christ, but the Spirit of God has taken up residence in our spirit, while Satan is somewhat handicapped by having to appeal to the selfish and sinful patterns in our soul. It is not a balanced, dualistic battle. It's a bit of an apples vs. oranges playing field, but don't feel bad for the devil.

Paul explains this inner conflict in Galatians 5:16,17 - "walk by the Spirit, and you will not carry out the desire of the flesh. For the flesh sets its desire against the Spirit, and the Spirit against the flesh; for these are in opposition to one another."

In much of popular Christian teaching, there seems to be a convoluted sense of interpretive dyslexia when they attempt to explain Gal. 5:16. They seem to think Paul wrote, "Do not carry out the desires of the flesh, and you will be walking by the Spirit." That is NOT how it reads!

The misinterpretation is based on the fact that "religion" always wants to cast the Christian life in terms of the self-effort of performance, what we allegedly need to DO to live Christianly. So, they focus on negative admonitions: "DO NOT carry out the desires of the flesh." "You need to suppress those desires, push them down, stuff them, smother them, and then you will be "walking by the Spirit" – by what you DO NOT DO.

Gal. 5:17 - "the flesh sets its desire against the Spirit, and the Spirit against the flesh; for these are in opposition to one another, so that you may not do the things that you please." There is an opposing and contrary orientation between the "desires of the flesh" and the desires of the Spirit of God. We do not want to diminish the fact that there is a conflict in the Christian life. BUT, we must note that it is the SPIRIT who sets its desires again the flesh. The power that will overcome the flesh does not come from us, but from the SPIRIT of GOD in us.

In large part, it comes down to "where is your focus" as you live the Christian life. Is your focus on your own ability to please God, or on the sufficiency of God's grace in Jesus Christ? "Not that we are sufficient/ adequate in ourselves, to consider anything as coming from ourselves, but our sufficiency/adequacy is from God" (II Cor. 3:5). We are "to fix our eyes on Jesus, the author and finisher of our faith" (Heb. 12:2).

Have you heard of the WYSIWYG principle? The acrostic stands for, "What You See Is What You Get!" This can be a physical principle: the seller may show you an object he is selling, and say, "what you see is what you get." "Inspect it, and determine if you want to buy it, in the condition it is in." But the WYSIWYG principle can also be applied to our spiritual focus. What we focus on, what we see, what looms large in the forefront of one's mind, what we concentrate on, and spend time thinking about, that is often going to be the direction of our action! When our attention is drawn to something, we are apt to be attracted to such, and follow that course of action. If our focus is on the selfishness and sinfulness of our flesh patternings, that is likely to be the way we "act out," with fleshly character in our behavior.

I have observed entire groups of Christians who seemed to be preoccupied with their "flesh," with understanding, identifying and comparing their "flesh patterns," and even explaining and excusing their "flesh patterns" as the basis of their personality. Such groups are often very "fleshly" in their interactions. The "deeds of the flesh" (Gal. 5:19-21) are often evident in their contentious bickerings and jealous jockeying for positions, and they are not a spiritual fellowship.

Conversely, I have found that in mature Christian groups, when their focus is on the sufficiency of the Lordship of Jesus Christ in their lives, when they understand the GRACE-dynamic of the indwelling Spirit of Christ in their lives, that they have "Christ in them, the hope of glory" (Col. 1:27), when their faith is focused on the living Lord Jesus, they are more likely to see and experience the life and character of the living Lord JESUS being lived out in them, "conformed to the image of the Son" (Rom. 8:29), and collectively exhibiting loving peace and harmony as the "Body of Christ."

This is not to say that we are attempting to project a perfect expression in the Christian life. Paul wrote, "Not that I am already perfect, but I press on toward the prize of the upward call of God in Christ Jesus" (Phil. 3:12-14). Every Christian has times when they misrepresent the One who is their Life, the One who lives in them as their identity, as a Christ-one. There will NEVER be a time in our Christian lives when "the flesh does not set its desire against the Spirit, and the Spirit against the flesh, in opposition to one another." There will never be a time in our Christian lives when we can cut the verses of Gal. 5:16,17 out of our Bibles, and say, "Those verses just aren't applicable to me anymore!"

Our focus must continually be on what Christ is doing in our lives, on His character expression in our behavior. With the "mind of Christ" (I Cor. 2:16) within us, we "set our minds on things above" (Col. 3:2); we set our minds "on God's interests" (Matt. 16:23).

II Pet. 1:4-11 - "4 For by these He has granted to us His precious and magnificent promises, so that by them you may become partakers of *the* divine nature, having escaped the corruption that is in the world by lust. 5 Now for this very reason also, applying all diligence, in your faith supply moral excellence, and in *your* moral excellence, knowledge, 6 and in *your* knowledge, self-control, and in *your* self-control, perseverance, and in *your* perseverance, godliness, 7 and in *your* godliness, brotherly kindness, and in *your* brotherly kindness, love. 8 For if these *qualities* are yours and are increasing, they render you neither useless nor unfruitful in the true knowledge of our Lord Jesus Christ. 9 For he who lacks these *qualities* is blind *or* short-sighted, having forgotten *his* purification from his former sins.
10 Therefore, brethren, be all the more diligent to make certain about His calling and choosing you; for as long as you practice these things, you will never stumble; 11 for in this way the entrance into the eternal kingdom of our Lord Savior Jesus Christ will be abundantly supplied to you."

Phil. 4:8 - "whatever is true, whatever is honorable, whatever is right, whatever is pure, whatever is lovely, whatever is of good repute, if there is any excellence and if anything is worthy of praise, think on these things."

As we think and focus on the things of Christ, the awareness of, and concern for the patterns of the "flesh" fade into the background of our consciousness. Those patterns are still there, but they are in the background of our awareness. We are always aware of our weaknesses, and propensities, and tendencies to go astray, but the POSITIVE of Christ in us is swallowing up the negatives of the "flesh." The "straight ways of God" (Acts 13:10) override the crooked, twisted, and warped patterns of the "flesh."

So, we have identified the Pauline concept of the "flesh" as "patterns of selfish and sinful character (Satan's character) in the God-given desires of our soul." We all have such individuated tendencies and propensities to selfishness. Every person's patterns of selfishness are distinctive and different from any other person's. Satan did his work in each of us, and we developed different patterns of how we individually and habitually act and react.

ALL these forms of self-effort with their patterned preconceptions and agendas will never pull-off the Christian life. They will only lead to frustration. They all fail to take into account our "unfathomable inclusion of participation in the very life of Jesus Christ. Jesus told His disciples, "Apart from ME, you can do nothing" (John 15:5), nothing that is godly or represents the divine character of God. I Thess. 5:24 – "Faithful is He who calls you, and He will bring it to pass. Gal. 2:20 – "It is no longer I who lives (the physical life and the Christian life), but Christ who lives in me, and the (Christian) life I now live, I live by faith in the Son of God (the receptivity of His activity)."

The Christian life is not a project to accomplish. It is not a promotional effort of fellowship. It is not a panacea to "calm the waters." It is not the propriety of belief and behavior. Rather, the Christian life is the PERSON of Jesus

Christ, His life lived out in and through us. II Cor. 3:5 – "we are not adequate in ourselves to consider anything as coming from ourselves, but our adequacy is from God."

The "seen" perspective is the natural human perspective. Our natural actions and reactions become the "affects" that torment our minds and emotions, affected with frustrations, irritations, discouragement, drudgery, monotony, despair, slogging through the "slough of despair" (*Pilgrim's Progress*), and despondency. We begin to sing the "poor me blues!" and want to withdraw into our own "pity-party."

The world of fallen mankind wallows in their reactions to the "seen," in the visible and visceral, in the apparent problems. The world of religion also is preoccupied with the "seen" reactions. Religion *thinks* like the world, *acts* like the world, and *evaluates* its results like the world. Religion is a worldly endeavor. Religion is the devil's playground.

Religion offers a false hope of getting beyond the trials and sorrows of life. "We are climbing Jacob's ladder, higher, higher." "I'm pressing on the upward way; new heights I'm gaining every day; Lord plant my feet on higher ground." Maturity is viewed as climbing toward a goal, and arriving at a summit top, living in the rarified air of "spirituality." Religion specializes in the "how-tos" of committed and dedicated climbing to attain maturity. Like the disciples of Jesus, we want to build three tabernacles on the mountain, and make ourselves at home in our perceived place of "spirituality."

On the other hand, religion offers a form of escapism, wanting to be delivered from this world, often encouraging isolationism, deliverance, and withdrawal from world. "This world is not my home, I'm just a passing through; my treasures are laid up somewhere beyond the blue; the angels beckon me from heaven's open door; I can't feel at home in this world anymore."

There are other perverted forms of religion, even those that seek the pain of masochism and hurt that might earn points with God. Religion tells people they need to "die to self," another form of masochism and performance, encouraging Christians to engage in self-crucifixion. What "self" do they advise we die to?

Religion thrives on the "seen" perspective. Religion is co-dependent to the problems and sins of the people. As long as people are buried in their problems, then they can be manipulated into attending, giving, and seeking the pseudo-solutions of religion in performance-oriented, legalistic activities.

Religion is full of advice, how-tos, and techniques alleged to show people how to identify, accommodate and overcome the "seen" circumstances. A common one is the encouragement to engage in "positive thinking," to "look at the bright side," to "keep your head up," "things will get better because everything comes to pass."

We have labelled the transition from the "seen" to the "unseen" as the *"Diaffective Process:" dia* = through; *affective* = situations of life that "affect" us internally and externally. We need to grasp the fact that we can move through the natural affective reactions to the "seen" circumstances of life to an "unseen" perspective whereby we can respond to what is happening around us by faith in God's activity.

The modern psychological community refers to "*Affective* Disorders," that involve the emotional reactions of guilt, shame, and anger. Such "Negative Affectivity," includes "neuroticism," depression, bipolar disorder, and anxiety disorder, including panic attacks, post-traumatic stress disorder, obsessive-compulsive disorder, etc. Affective disorders are also thought to include attention-deficit disorder, bulimia nervosa, hyper-sexuality, kleptomania, and others. An *affective* disorder is diagnosed when an individual has developed a pattern of indulging in, or denying the existence of, how the situations of life "affect" them. The natural affectations to life's circumstances may be quite variable (high/low; on again/off again; passive/ aggressive), and psychology refers to such as "affective lability" (variability). (cf. *Diagnostic and Statistical Manual of Mental Disorders*. Fifth Edition. DSM-5, published by American Psychiatric Association.)

Psychology also speaks of "*Disaffective* Disorders" (also referred to as "restricted" or "blunted affectivity"), such as apathy, antipathy, lethargy, alienation, withdrawal, torpor, inertia, sloth, aversion, discontent, listlessness, inaction, isolationism, or the adolescent resignation of "whatever." In this condition, a person may deny and "check out" from reacting or allowing circumstances to "affect" them by insulating or isolating themselves, "pulling into a shell," "going under the covers," burrowing into their own personal rabbit-hole.

It is important to understand what we are referring to as the "*Diaffective* Process," wherein we see "through" and move "through" the natural, reactive psychological "affects" that are so common to humans as they react to life here on earth, in order to see and experience the "unseen" perspective of God at work in the midst of those same situations.

This *"Diaffective* Process" might be illustrated historically by the Israelites, going through the many trials of the wilderness for forty years before they could experience the Promised Land. Constantly, they had to be reminded, "The way out is through!" We all spend a lot of time in the wilderness of the "seen" perspective, employing numerous natural reactions, before we begin to "see" with spiritually enlightened eyes what God is up to in our lives, and begin to experience the "promised land" of God's abundant spiritual blessings in our lives.

Often the "seen" perspective and experience is where we "hit the wall," where we seem to "run out of options" for how we think we can handle life and control our circumstances. We come to the end of our "logical alternatives to faith." Remember Abraham's other son, Ishmael? That was Abraham's "logical alternative to faith." It seems that we hard-headed humans have to learn in the school of hard-knocks, and finally get it through our heads what does not work, so we will begin to long for what does work in dealing with life. As Burt Rosenberg has said, "You have to know what *ain't* in order to know what *IS*." The IS is always in the I AM, the One who IS, and is in control of all things, including every facet of our lives.

Another biblical example of attempting to handle life's situations with the self-sufficiency by which we react in the "seen" dimension of natural thought and action, might be the prophet Jonah. Running away from his call to go to Nineveh, he found himself tossed overboard from a ship and swallowed by a large fish. He ran out of options on the "seen" level of alternatives. What else could he do, but allow God to act on his behalf, and submit to what God had called him to do by means of the unseen provision of God's enabling?

Some readers may be acquainted with Dan Stone and his ministry. Perhaps you have read his book, *The Rest of the Gospel*. Dan often used an illustration he called "the line." That line, as he explained it, was an invisible line between the "seen" and the "unseen." The "line" illustration was used to distinguish and differentiate between two different perspectives, not two realms, but two perspectives on what is going on as we live in the world, the temporal perspective and the eternal perspective.

Some people were confused by the illustration of "the line," because Dan often referred to "above the line" and "below the line" as if they were two different places. In reality, there are simply two perspectives, points of view/reference (the seen and the unseen), and they are always simultaneous. People tend to bounce from one to the other, like a ping-pong ball.

Dan Stone explained, "There's really no such thing as a line. These two realms (*perspectives*) coexist. The unseen and eternal is going on in the midst of the seen and temporal. As believers, we have the privilege of living an unseen and eternal life in the midst of this seen and temporal world."

We are emphasizing what is involved in "seeing through to the unseen," what we have called the "*Diaffective* Process" of moving through the natural and inevitable human reactions to the experiences that are going on around us at all times, and recognizing that we have the inner resource and treasure of the Spirit of Christ dwelling in our spirit in the midst of every situation. We have what it takes (every Christian has what it takes) to move into the counterintuitive perspective of "seeing God" in all situations and participating with God as we allow for the receptivity of His activity by FAITH. We have the privilege to be "in on what God is up to!"

The question is: Can we (will we), because Jesus Christ lives in us, allow for a *"diaffective* process" that "moves through" the natural affects and reactions, and simultaneously experiences the counterintuitive perspective of the "unseen," with the God-inspired, God energized character that is concerned about "others," and desires to KNOW God relationally to the fullest extent possible.

THE UNSEEN PERSPECTIVE

Time for a little personal confession here! I have struggled in my preparation to know how to articulate and share this category of the "unseen." The reality of the "unseen" perspective cannot be systematized, categorized or proceduralized. It does not fit my logical brain patterns; it puts my mind in a tail-spin; it stretches me beyond the capability of my natural tools. The dynamics of the "unseen" is novel and unique in every Christian individual. It cannot be explained in any "how-tos," in any nice, neat boxes of explanation, complete with diagrams (as I am so prone to do).

Paul explained, "The ways of God are past finding out" (Rom. 11:33 - KJV); they are unsearchable, inscrutable, inexplicable, beyond human understanding; they cannot be put into human words.

No matter what I say, or how I explain it, I cannot take you there, as if this were a place that could be conceptualized as a destination. I feel inadequate to introduce you to this perspective, to this outlook, to this "point of view" on God and life. Only the Lord Jesus Christ can take the one in whom He dwells to this place of understanding and experience. But I am convinced that this is where He wants to lead us, and share with us, and commune and fellowship with us! He desires to be our "spiritual director," to lead us into Himself.

All I can do is try to point you to a perspective that I know is real, and God wants us to participate in – in **HIM**. All I can be is a "herald" of a "holy place" of God's presence and power that God has prepared for us in the temple of His presence.

"He who has ears to hear, let him hear what the Spirit is saying" (Mk 4:23; 7:16; Rev. 2,3). He who has eyes to see, let him develop the spiritual vision, enlightenment, illumination, and revelation to see from God's perspective.

To "see the unseen," we have to develop divine sensitivities, to be attuned to sensing and experiencing the heart of God. These are "things which eye has not seen and ear has not heard, and which have not entered the heart of man, all that God has prepared for those who love Him" (I Cor. 2:9).

Knowing God's heart in the "unseen" perspective is a spiritual reality that only a genuine, legitimate, truly born-again Christian can ever know. The non-Christian will only consider it a ridiculous non-scientific cop-out, idle speculations and fantasies, taking flight into ethereal mind-games. The "god of this age has blinded the minds of the unbelievers" (II Cor. 4:4), and they are unable to comprehend the "unseen" perspective. The natural man cannot understand spiritual things (I Cor. 2:14).

Only the Christian can recognize that "navigating in the seen" perspective is always blurred with self-concern and self-aspiration; contaminated with selfish fleshly patterns. Many who identify themselves as "Christians" never get there! As discerning Christians, we recognize that in the "seen" arena we "see through a glass darkly" (I Cor. 13:12), often thinking that we've got it all figured out, logically and scientifically and psychologically. But those who have seen God's perspective in the "unseen," can look back with 20/20 hindsight and "see" that the difficult experiences of life, as hard as they might have been, were "the best thing that ever happened to them!"

"It was the path God used to allow me to take my eyes off of myself and to see Him." I have heard many Christians testify, "Despite how difficult it was, I wouldn't trade it for anything."

It's a process of learning to listen to the voice of God. Jesus said, "My sheep hear My voice" (Jn. 10:16,27). It takes time and experiences to learn to recognize God's voice and direction in our lives. But that is the basis of new covenant Christian "obedience." Christian obedience is not "keeping rules," trying to obey the Law. New covenant obedience is based on the Greek word *hupakouo*, to "listen under." Rules and regulations are irrelevant, for we are involved in intimate personal relationship. As C.S. Lewis says, "legalistic obedience is a joke," it is not how a Christian understands "obedience." Ours is a relational obedience, the "obedience of faith" (Rom. 1,16), the obedience of love! Christian obedience is "listening under" the directive voice of the Spirit of Christ in order to ascertain the next opportunity to respond in faith to what He wants to do in our lives.

The perspective of the "unseen" is perceived only by divine revelation. This divine revelation is caught, not taught! It is an inner teaching. Listen again to the words of Dan Stone,

> "Until the Holy Spirit tells us, God's unseen and eternal realities seem to be outside of us. So, we set out to gain information about them, thinking that if we gain enough information, we can produce the spiritual life. Some of us have garnered entire libraries to help us gain the spiritual life, and what we ended up with was not much spiritual life, but lots of information about it. Unfortunately, there's no relationship between the amount of information we accumulate and the ability to live a spiritual life. But there

is a direct correlation between the amount of information we gain and our level of frustration. In the things of the Spirit, no amount of know-about gives you the ability to do. The only One who can live the Christian life is Christ. It is the goodness of God to let us be frustrated until we are open to His revelation of Himself and His sufficiency. Without that revelation, we're not going to have an experiential understanding of the unseen and eternal realities that are ours in Christ Jesus."

It is not mental comprehension gained by human teaching that we need. It is not cerebral education and understanding that we need to go beyond the "seen" circumstances. Instead of trying to "*understand*," we need simply to "*stand under*" the Lordship of Jesus Christ and the empowering of the Holy Spirit, and respond to His direction.

The "unseen" is the perspective wherein one knows that they are loved by God, wherein we really know beyond a shadow of doubt that we are God's beloved. We know such not with our brain, but with the relational presence of the triune God in our heart. It is similar to the difference between a mental knowing about marriage and the intimate "knowing" of one's spouse in a marital relationship (cf. Gen. 4:1).

Christians have long desired to know the "acceptance" of God in Christ. Paul explained to the Ephesians that we are "accepted in the beloved" (Eph. 2:6), but we must go beyond the objectivity of such a statement to the point where we are subjectively convinced that "the Lord will never forsake or reject us" (Heb. 13:5). It is in the "unseen" perspective we experience personal and spiritual "intimacy" with God. The older Christian writers of a few centuries ago used to call it "intercourse" with God.

This "unseen" perspective does not come naturally. It is *counter-intuitive, counter-cultural* and *counter-productive* to the functional operations of the world around us. It is a supernatural reality that we cannot orchestrate, but can only participate in because the life of Jesus lives in us, and the Holy Spirit is at work in our lives.

It is in this "unseen" perspective that we begin to experience what it means to swim in the sea of God's **LOVE**. As we do so, we understand that the Love of God is always directed toward OTHERS. We develop empathy for others, a deep-seated internal concern that the narcissistic world knows nothing about, because their perspective is, "It's all about ME!" The word "empathy" is derived from two Greek words, *em* = in; *pathy* = pathos. The Christian is "in pathos" with another, feeling what they feel, uniting with the other in their painful struggle, identifying with their hurt, willing to stand vicariously in their place as an intercessor.

It is in this "unseen" perspective that we can begin to live out of our spiritual identity "in Christ." This is who I really am! I want to live in the environment that I am suited for and designed to function within. We want to behave like who we've become in Christ.

We are new creatures, with a new character. We can begin to allow that character of Christ in the core of our spirit-being to permeate our attitude and emotions, and flow out in behavior. In our human spirit, we have the *character* of the spirit-person who inhabits our deepest being. In the functionality of our soul, we develop *attitudes* that are formed from the character of the one who dwells in our spirit. In our physical bodies, we express and manifest the *behavior* that exemplifies the character of the indwelling spirit within.

The "unseen" realities are not outside of us, or exterior to us, something to be sought; rather the reality of everything "unseen" is in the Person of Jesus Christ who lives in every Christian person. We will never find the "unseen" in the "seen" and tangible world outside of us.

Spiritual maturity is growing in the perspective that "sees *through*" the unpleasantries of life to see the sufficiency of Christ in everything, to see the goodness of God at work in the lives of His people – in the lives of all people! We begin to see the patient faithfulness of God to bring all people along at the pace they can endure.

The "unseen" perspective begins to see the absolute "purity" of God's character. Soren Kierkegaard explained, "purity of heart is to will one thing, to seek the simple, what is wholly integrated with God," "to love God with all your heart, soul, mind, and strength" (Mk. 12:30).

Here we begin to experience the "ecstasy" of God, and it doesn't take a pill to bring that ecstatic experience. The word "ecstasy" comes from two Greek words, *ek* = out of; *stasis* = to stand, so spiritual ecstasy is "to stand out from the world." Here it is that we begin to "live in the heavenly places" (Eph. 1:3; 2:6; 6:12). Here we begin to "mount up with wings like eagles" (Isa. 40:32; Exod. 19:4), and seem to soar and float in the Spirit. At Pentecost, those around them thought they were intoxicated.

The "unseen" perspective is where we are lifted up to live by and in the resurrection-life of Jesus, the out-lived re-presentation of the Christ-life. There we experience a rising above the "stuff" that threatens to sink us in the "seen" perspective. We have the privilege of living by the life of Christ in such a way that Christ "is our life." (Col. 3:4).

The "unseen" perspective is participation in the "transcendent life." Christians have "tasted of the heavenly gift" (Heb. 6:4), are partakers of the Holy Spirit (Heb. 6:4), have been enlightened (Heb. 6:4; Eph. 1:18) by the Spirit, and their eyes have been opened to the ways of God. The "unseen" is the perspective wherein we experience "walking by the Spirit" (Gal. 5:16), and "living by the Spirit" (Gal. 5:25).

From the "unfathomable participation" that Christians have in the very life of the risen Lord Jesus, we have the privilege of being integrated in the heavenly oneness of intimacy with the Trinity – Father, Son, and Holy Spirit. In that place, the "holy place" of intimate relation with the triune God of the universe, that is where we find that all of the contrasts and contradictions fade away into insignificance. It is a place of perfect oneness, free of imperfections. "He who is joined to the Lord is one spirit with Him" (I Cor. 6:17).

Christians have long placed so much attention on pinning down one's relational security with God. Elaborate formulas have been developed for surety of proper belief and engaging in acceptable procedures of initiation. Theories of "once saved, always saved" have been constructed to provide mental certainty for skeptical Christians. As we participate in the "unseen" communion with Father, Son, and Holy Spirit, we realize that genuine spiritual security is in **JESUS** alone; knowing that we are His, and He will keep us and "perfect us until the day of Christ Jesus" (Phil. 1:6) and the consummation of all things in Him.

True contentment is found in the "unseen" awareness that God supplies all our needs. In that context, Paul could say, "I have learned to be content in whatever circumstances I am" (Phil. 4:11). It is here that the Christ-one can relax, let down their guard, and "rest" (cf. Matt. 11:28,29; Heb. 4:1-11) in God's provision and sufficiency. Such contentment can even accept the external insults, difficulties (II Cor. 12:10), persecution (Jn. 15:20), and sufferings (Acts 9:16) of life. With this perspective, we can "share in the sufferings of Jesus" (Phil. 3:10; Col. 1:24, I Pet. 4:13; 5:1), counting such to be a privilege that leads to the extension of God's glory.

This is the perspective wherein we recognize God's sufficiency, and live in the sufficiency of God's GRACE – allowing God to BE and DO what God wants to BE and DO – going with the flow of God's GRACE. We begin to "see God at work" in our lives. "My grace is sufficient for you; My power is made perfect in weakness" (II Cor. 12:9). "We have all sufficiency for everything" (II Cor. 9:8). "Our sufficiency is from Him" (II Cor. 3:5).

The "unseen" is the experience of living by FAITH – the receptivity of God's activity of Grace. Faith is much more than believing the correct tenets of doctrinal teaching, and much more than a personal resolve to live as God would have us to live. Faith is our privilege to allow God's character to be manifest in our behavior (II Cor. 4:10,11), serving as the conduits of God's activity.

Real "repentance" occurs in the "unseen." Repentance is not changing one's behavior for the better, nor just "changing one's mind" about our belief-system. Repentance is not just remorse for what we've done, nor "turning over a new leaf" in a lifestyle remodel. Repentance (Greek *metanoia*) is a "change of mind that leads to a change of action." Change of mind entails the recognition that "I can't; I don't have what it takes to pull this Christian life off, to be an overcomer in life. I've butted my head against the wall for long enough, I admit my personal inability." BUT I have to believe that there is something/someone greater than me (a higher power) that CAN be the One who brings control and stability to my life, that CAN be "Lord" of my life, that can take charge. And I choose to let Him; I freely choose to allow Him to implement a change of action, a new course of response to the circumstances of life, and to rely on His sufficiency. I CAN'T; HE CAN; I will choose to LET HIM control my life, depending on Him and deriving all from Him. This is a repetitive and continuous process of repentance – not just an initial response at conversion, but a life of repentance. "*I can't* live life as God desires for me; *HE can* live His life in me; *I want* to keep on allowing Him to do so."

Thomas Aquinas once wrote, "Man cannot live without joy; when he is deprived of spiritual joys, he will necessarily be addicted to carnal pleasures." Without finding JOY in the "unseen" realities of the living Lord Jesus, human beings will revert to the "seen" pleasures of fleshliness. Spiritual joy is far more than emotional exuberance and euphoria. The Greek word for "joy" is *chara*, derived from the Greek word for "grace," *charis*. The deepest sense of joy comes in the experience of God's grace, not in the selfish quest for the chance happiness that "everything is going my way." James even explains, "Count it all JOY, my brethren, when you encounter various trials" (James 1:2), knowing that God's grace will be operative. "My joy shall be in you, and your joy shall be made full" (Jn. 15:11), Jesus told His disciples.

The apostle Peter wrote, "You are protected by the power of God through faith for a salvation ready to be revealed in the last time. In this you greatly rejoice, even though now for a little while, if necessary, you have been distressed by various trials, so that the proof of your faith, being more precious than gold which is perishable, even though tested by fire, may be found to result in praise and glory and honor at the revelation of Jesus Christ; and though you have not seen Him (the "unseen" perspective), you love Him, and though you do not see Him now ("unseen), but believe in Him, you greatly rejoice with JOY inexpressible and full of glory, obtaining as the outcome of your faith the salvation of your souls" (I Pet. 1:5-9). There is great JOY in the "unseen" realities of the Christ-life that transcends all the trials of life.

The "unseen" experience is the perspective and experience of PEACE. Such "peace" is not the absence of conflict or the absence of problems, but the settled assurance that God is at work in the midst of every circumstance. Jesus said, "Peace I leave with you; My peace I give to you; not as the world gives do I give to you. Do not let your heart be troubled, nor let it be fearful" (Jn. 14:27). In the "unseen" perspective we realize that "God is not a God of confusion, but of peace" (I Cor. 14:33), and "the mind set on the Spirit is life and peace." (Rom. 8:6). "The peace of God, which surpasses all comprehensive, will guard your hearts and minds in Christ Jesus" (Phil. 4:7).

Participating in the "unseen" allows us to experience the "will of God." The will of God is not some objective goal that we are looking for. The will of God is **JESUS**, and the joy of living in Him.

When we are participating in the "unseen" perspective, we are able to see the situations of life as God's opportunities – not obstacles thrown in our path. We want to "see God" at work in every situation (Rom. 8:28). "Yes, Lord, I want to be *in on* what You're *up to!*"

Have you ever stopped to think that "God doesn't have any problems!" Just opportunities to exhibit His sufficiency in all things. The English word "problem" comes from two Greek words: *pro* = before; *ballo* = to throw. Human problems are just situations that are "thrown in front of us" to provide the opportunity to demonstrate that "we have what it takes" in Jesus Christ to let His character shine through.

The "seen" perspective sees the problems of life as obstacles. In faith, we see them as opportunities. The natural perspective of the "seen" sees them as tragedies, whereas with the faith of the "unseen" we see them as "trajectories." In the "seen" perspective we are always recounting our "problems," but in faith we can see them as "springboards." What some call "catastrophes" can be viewed in the "unseen" as "catapults." The "trials" of life can be viewed as "tests" of God to see whether we will see Christ and His sufficiency in the midst of the situations.

The Christian should be able to see external problems as but "the speed bumps" of life, the means by which God gets our attention to cause us to "see beyond the seen" in order to see what He is "up to," what He wants to be and do next in our lives. When we are able to accept the situation before us, rather than reacting negatively, we are able to say, "OK Lord, where is this situation going? Take it where you will, and I will trust in your sufficiency."

The "unseen" is the perspective of genuine and real thanksgiving. Eph. 5:20 – "giving thanks for all things." I Thess. 5:18 – "in everything give thanks". The Greek word for "giving thanks" is *eucharisteuo*, the word from which we get Eucharist. That is why we call the Lord's Supper "*Eucharist*" - because Jesus took the bread and "gave thanks." *Eu-charist* comes from two Greek words, *eu* = good; *charis* = grace. To "give thanks" is to recognize the "good grace" of God. In the "unseen" perspective, we begin to see the "good grace" of God in all things and "give thanks" for all things. The whole of our lives becomes a eucharistic experience. This may sound strange, but I have even learned to let a bowel movement become a eucharistic experience. "Thank you, Lord, for letting my plumbing work as You designed." Someone might ask, "Can you thank God for the devil?" The depth of spiritual relationality requires freedom of choice. Genuine freedom of choice requires an alternative option. God saw fit to allow Satan to be the alternative option!

In the realm and perspective of the "unseen," we recognize that PRAYER is more than saying words to God. Prayer becomes the simplicity of simply saying, "Yes, Lord!" Even in the midst of temptation we can say, "Yes, Lord, YOU are my all, and all I need in this situation." "Thank you, Lord, for the opportunity to see your sufficiency!" We can experience what it means to "pray without ceasing."

The "unseen" is to participate in the "secret place" (Matt. 6:6) that Jesus spoke of, where we commune with God in the unity and oneness of prayer. It is the "love chamber," where we meet with "the Lover of our soul," the "divine beloved." It is not a tangible place or material place, but it is the place that is formed by our relationship with the triune God, the place where we are "near to the heart of God" (cf. hymn by Cleland McAfee), the place where we open up to allow God to do whatever He wants to do, and consent to derive all from Him.

The "unseen" perspective is the experience of "kingdom living." Jesus came declaring, "The kingdom of God is at hand. It is here!" "The kingdom of God/heaven is in your midst. It is within you" (Lk. 17:21). We have been given the "mystery of the kingdom" (Mk. 4:11). Many conceive the "kingdom" to be a realm, a tangible entity expected in the future, perhaps in Jerusalem. The kingdom is a Person! The kingdom is JESUS – nothing more! Jesus is the KING that constitutes the Kingdom! When He is serving as King of Kings and Lord of Lords in the kingdom of our hearts and lives, then we are participating in kingdom-living. Yes, it is unseen; there is no tangible throne, but Jesus wants to "reign" in our lives.

The manifestation of the holy character of God occurs in the "unseen" perspective. The Greek word for "holiness" is *hagiasmos*. Scottish Bible teacher, William Barclay, noted that any word ending in *–asmos* refers to a process. It doesn't happen all at once, but Christ is our sanctification (I Cor. 1:30), as we participate in the transformational, conformational process of Christian living.

It is here that we begin to participate in what we were created to be. Created in the image of God, to manifest the glory of God. We allow for the visible expression of the invisible God – NOT just the representation or reflection, but the real expression of God's character.

In the midst of the "unseen", the burden of God's heart to love others and share the only provision for Life in Jesus is laid upon us. Yes, the living Lord Jesus is within us, but "Christ in us" is always "Christ for others," not merely to make us fat and spiritually bloated. The loving heart of God for others will weigh heavy upon us. We recognize that genuine ministry is just the overflow of Jesus in us into the lives of others.

ETERNAL WEIGHT OF GLORY

The "eternal weight of glory" is NOT something in the future, put off until we get to heaven. It is a reality that can be experienced "here and now." Paul explained that we have "Christ in us, the hope of glory" – not just heavenly glory, but the confident expectation of manifesting God's glorious character presently, moment by moment, unto His own glory (Col. 1:27).

Christians are to be open and available to the "eternal weight of God's GLORY," as He conforms us to Himself. Paul explained that "momentary, light affliction (the experiences of life) is producing for us an *eternal weight of glory* far beyond all comparison, while we look not at the things which are *seen*, but at the things which are *not seen*; for the things which are *seen* are *temporal*, but the things which are *not seen* are *eternal*" (II Cor. 4:17,18).

This is what we were created for as human beings – "created for His glory" (Isa. 43:7). But remember, He does not "give His glory to another" (Isa. 42:8; 48:11); His glory is the manifestation of His all-glorious character in His creation, and we cannot manufacture or produce that. It has to be God in Christ by the Spirit expressing Himself, and we have to allow Him to do so by the receptivity of faith. I Cor. 10:31 – "Do all to the glory of God." As stated in the Westminster Confession: "The chief end of man is to glorify God and enjoy Him forever."

The original meaning of the Hebrew word (*kabod*) that we translate as "glory" has a basic meaning of "to be heavy" or "to weigh upon" – "weight" or "heaviness." When we are in the presence of the glory of God and we are aware of it, we become conscious of something greater than ourselves pressing upon us, crowding and weighing on us, like a heavy (yet not oppressive) spiritual presence. The presence of the character of God reveals everything other than God to be of light-weight consequence, mere "fluff" compared to the weight of God's presence and glory.

Like the *Shekinah* glory in the Holy Place of the tabernacle and temple, God's presence is an unimaginable glory that can only be explained as an unbearable light.

In experiential terms, the presence of God's character "presses" us into Himself. Perhaps we might explain it as God's "bear-hug," the divine squeeze, the relational embrace of the loving God. That is what we all desire at the deepest core of our being – the embrace of God's eternal LOVE, pressing us into Himself, pulling us into Himself, and "pressing us" to be the manifestations of His glorious character by the "fruit of the Spirit" (Gal. 5:22,23) in whatever circumstance we might find ourselves. We might refer the "weight of glory" as God's "spiritual pressure." The divine pressure that we might be "conformed to the image of Jesus Christ" (Rom. 8:29). God is using the experiences of life and the awareness of His powerful grace-sufficiency to do just that!

Everything is intended to be compressed into one thing only – JESUS, the Divine Being, the ultimate and only Reality, and our presence in His presence. Christ in us, the expectation of glory! (Col. 1:27).

This experience with God is so glorious that we run out of words to explain the reality. That's why some Christians have yielded to the temptation of overstatement, using mystical metaphors that would seem to imply that they have been deified or absorbed into the Godhead. It is important, however, to "stay grounded" in the theological and ideological undergirding of Christian experience, so we don't float away into fantasy-land.

There are times when we might sense that we "are soaring on wings like eagles" (Isa. 40:31). There are times when we feel like we're going to burst like an overfilled balloon with joy, love, peace, and the ecstasy of Christ's life. There are times when Christians feel as if we are just floating in the buoyancy of God's grace, in a euphoria of delight. As the Christian chorus states, "If it keeps getting better and better, O Lord, I don't know what I'm going to do!"

BUT, I have found that God doesn't usually let us soar in the rarified air too long. The glory-floating is fleeting! WHY? God wants us to get our feet on the ground again. We live in this world for a reason, and it is not that we should be so heavenly-minded, that we are of no earthly good. God is LOVE, and He wants us to be the vessels that share His LOVE with "others." Christ lives in us for "others." That's what LOVE is! It is the opposite of selfishness and self-striving! LOVE is always other-oriented.

Christians are always "sent ones" (Jn. 17:18). We are "ambassadors" (II Cor. 5:20). We are "lovers" expressing God's love. We are intercessors, making intercession before God for "others," willing to "stand in the gap" for OTHERS. That means we have to get involved with others in the "muck" of life here on earth. God's specializes in bringing life out of death, good out of evil, light out of darkness, and we are the instruments through which he wants to evidence and share such.

Christians are the letter, the epistle of Christ to the world around us. Paul explained to the Corinthian Christians, "you are our letter, written in our hearts, known and read by all men, ... the letter of Christ" (II Cor. 3:2,3). We are the only expression of "Christ" that some people will ever encounter. People will see Christ in us, Christ through us, Christ *as* us. Yes, we are "the epistle of Joe, or Sue, or Mary" to those around us.

We are witnesses of the work of God in our lives. The Greek word for "witness" is *marture*, we are those who are willing to "lay down our lives" for others, as martyrs exhibiting God's character through us. It is often through our dying, through our experience of the cross-life, that others see Jesus. They see that the Christ-life really works, no matter how tough the going gets!

In Christian ministry, the life of Jesus in the Christian begins to overflow into the lives of others. Christian ministry is not a profession, a position, or a job. Christian ministry is not a matter of trying to save the world by convincing others to believe in Jesus. It is living out the life of Jesus in such a way that others want what (Who) we have.

There have been (and are) some Christians who have sought to be ascetics and mystics. They desire to live in a state of euphoric perfect God-consciousness continuously. They want to get beyond all the physical experiences and problems of life here on earth. The problem is, they take the problems with them wherever they go. They still have the "flesh" patterns. Even in the cave, or the monastery, they find that there is "a mouse in the house" – the rat has built his nesting patterns within us!

Looking again at the "big picture" of our "house of contrats, it might be noted that the foundational *either/ors* provide the antitheses of the cosmic forces of the universe. The contrasts of the dialectic *both/ands* provide the tensioned balance of the interactives of human thought. And the experiential reaction or response of the *"seen" and "unseen"* provides the perspectives whereby some sense can be made of the whole process of human living.

We must admit that the entire illustration of the Christian House of Contrasts is "outside of the box" of traditional religious thought, with its emphasis on correct doctrines, pragmatic church operations, acceptable ethical and moral behavior, etc.

We are not saying that a perspective gained from the Christian House of Contrasts will allow one to have everything figured out with finite human understanding. The fullness of what God is doing remains a "mystery." God's presence and God's ways are always beyond our ability to comprehend. But, I think this illustration provides (for me, anyway) a focal point, a perspective, some insight into the meaningful trajectory of life here on earth, i.e. what life's all about!

Where does the Church enter into this discussion? I do think that an awareness of the simultaneity of the "seen" and the "unseen" perspectives in our lives should reveal to us what the Church of Jesus Christ was meant to be. The Church is Christian people, who have the same kinds of experiences that all human beings have, and they gather and assemble together as brothers and sisters in Christ, to interact and encourage one another in the Christ-life and the process of "moving through" our natural human reactions via the *diaffective process*.

(1) In those gatherings, we are meant to honestly and transparently admit that we have a whole complex pattern of natural tendencies to respond to life's experiences with natural reactions of self-concern. Christians need to "open up" and share their failures. We Christians do not begin to be as honest as the addicts in the anonymity meetings, ex. Alcoholics Anonymous, Narcotics Anonymous, Sexaholics Anonymous. Many stay in their shell until they come to those times when they come to the end of our rope and spill all in the counselor's office. Christians are meant to interact together with honesty and transparency. James 5:16 – we are to "confess our sins to one another, and pray for one another," to "admonish one another" (Rom. 15:14; Col. 3:16), to accept one another" (Rom. 15:7), to "bear one another's burden" (Gal. 6:2), to "show tolerance for one another" (Eph. 4:2), to "build one another up" (Rom. 14:19; I Thess. 5:11)), to "comfort one another" (I Thess. 4:18), to "encourage one another" (I Thess. 5:11; Heb. 3:13; 10:25), and to "love one another" (Jn. 13:34,35; Ro. 13:8; I Thess. 3:12). The Church is to be the community of the interactive "one anothers." That means that we share and commiserate with one another about our natural, fallen, selfish tendencies to react to life's experiences from the perspective of the "seen." We need to see each other in the process of repentance, wherein we admit that "We can't," only HE can, and we want Him to manifest the lived-out character of God in us. We have to be honest! That doesn't mean that we gather together for

an orgy of sin-conscious confession of all our base desires, but we cannot function as the organic "Body of Christ," the Church, unless we are transparently invested in each other's lives, so as to know how to pray for one another, especially about our short-sighted reactions from the "seen" perspective.

(2) On the other hand, when Christians gather and assemble together we are meant to "encourage one another" (I Thess. 5:11) by sharing our times when we were able to see beyond or through the "seen" natural reactions or "affects" of our experiences and respond in faith; those times when we have "listened to the Spirit in obedience" and heard the voice of Jesus Christ our shepherd; when we have been assured that we are loved and accepted by the Beloved, and God has revealed how He wants to work in our lives. We need to share those times when we have acted out of our identity in Christ, and behaved like who we've become in Him, by allowing His life to be manifested in our daily situations. Every genuine Christian experiences these times of spiritual victory and triumph, these times when we transcend the "seen," experience a spiritual "high," when we submit to the abundant grace of God in Christ (I Tim. 1:14), see Him working more abundantly than we could ask or think, according to His power at work within us (Eph. 3:20), and delight in the "abundant life" (Jn. 10:10) that Jesus promised. God's GRACE is at work in our lives. You know it is, and I know it is, and we need to share our delights and victories. But the tempter doesn't want us to delight in God's grace-times; he wants us to focus on the "seen" reactions when we focused on ourselves and our perceived sad plight, rather than on the sufficiency and victory that are ours in Christ.

So, why hasn't the Church been functioning as the "Body of Christ?" Why haven't we experienced the collective and interactive function of the life of Jesus Christ in our assemblies? In large part, it is because we have sacrificed our sense of "one another" involvement. We have allowed "church" to become an educational institution wherein a pastor/teacher attempts to dump doctrinal information into people's mind for 30-45 minutes a week, accept contributions for so doing, and then function as a cheerleader-promoter to goad the people to more involvement, while masochistically berating the people for not doing enough. If that continues, the institutional church will be "dead as a dodo bird" within the next century, for it is already sliding down the slippery-slop into irrelevancy! Attendance is declining in the traditional churches across America, and we have become a laughing-stock in the culture of our society.

Genuine interactive Christian assembly, the real *ecclesia*, must be an honest "one another" sharing of our continuing "seen" reactions and our "unseen" faith responses, wherein we love one another and the world of hurting people around us with the LOVE of God in Christ by the Spirit. Thereby, we encourage one another (cf. Heb. 10:25) to "move through" the "seen" reactions to earthly life, and the exercise of a faith response whereby we are receptive to the "unseen" workings of God through the Spirit of Christ.

I think it is important for Christians to recognize how these experiential "seen" and "unseen" perspectives relate to the practical interaction of what we call "church."

There is a sense in which this entire "unseen" perspective is beyond what we humans are able to communicate, beyond human communication categories which are limited to space/time context. The "unseen" is inarticulable, inexplicable, an inexpressible perspective, and yet, by the unfathomable inclusion in the life of the living Lord Jesus, it has been given to us, is "in us," and is meant to be lived out through us.

The James B. Phillips translation of Col. 1:9-13 explains the process quite well:

> "We are asking God that you may see things, as it were, from His point of view (perspective) by being given spiritual insight and understanding. We also pray that your outward lives, which men see, may bring credit to your master's name, and that you may bring joy to his heart by bearing genuine Christian fruit, and that your knowledge of God may grow yet deeper. As you live this new life, we pray that you will be strengthened from God's boundless resources, so that you will find yourselves able to pass through any experience and endure it with courage. You will even be able to thank God in the midst of pain and distress because you are privileged to share the lot of those who are living in the light. For we must never forget that he rescued us from the power of darkness, and re-established us in the kingdom of his beloved Son, that is, in the kingdom of light."

Please do not think that I have this "unseen" perspective mastered (no one does!), that my sharing of what I know of this spiritual mind-set constitutes a high level of "spirituality." I'm just a newbie, a novice, a neophyte in the process of setting my mind on the "unseen" things of the Spirit. I spend far more time that I want to admit in the natural "seen" perspective, caught up in the "me–mindset" of self-concern, unable to see beyond the end of my own nose.

We all spend more time in the "seen" perspective than we want to admit. We react, and our emotional well-being is adversely affected. There are times of bitterness, personal hurt, fear, anger, discouragement, worry, etc. I think it is inevitable as long as we are human beings living in this world. But, there can be a simultaneous perspective of the "seen" and the "unseen." I do not know of anyone who has achieved the level of faith that they live in continual Christ-consciousness. In fact, I think that if anyone could/would ever reach such an alleged state of consciousness and perspective, God would make sure to plant their feet on the ground again in another difficult situation that threatened their status-quo, and they, as well as others, could observe their natural reaction. Some Christians are quite appalled at the regularity of their natural reactions and failure to "see through the human affects" and participate in the "unseen." Some engage in excessive confession and alarm: "God, I have lapsed into the "seen" again. Can You believe it? And God's response always seems to be, "I didn't expect anything else out of you, for apart from the response of faith that allows for the receptivity of My character activity in you in the midst of the situation, you will time and time again continue to react with fleshliness and a selfish perspective. And we do! Over and over again! Don't beat yourself up about it. Don't be a masochist. Don't let the religious leaders send you on guilt trips about it. Just keep your eyes on Jesus and enjoy the times when by God's grace you do "see beyond" and glimpse the transcendent reality of His life and character while your feet are still planted on planet earth, in the world.

We may desire the unhindered perfection and enjoyment of Christ's life here on earth on a permanent and continual basis, but if we were to experience such totally and continuously we would lose our sense of hope and expectation for what God has for us in the future. Yet, we must always recognize that He has nothing for us that He hasn't already provided for us in Jesus.

I do not think that anyone who begins to experience the "unseen" perspective of God's function in them and the world around them, will ever feel like they have really "entered in" fully to God's presence. They will always feel like they have just stepped into the vast beauty, depth, and intensity of this perspective, "near to the heart of God." They have just glimpsed an expanding panorama, just put their toe into the vast ocean of God's bounteous sufficiency. I know that I feel like a little infant lying on the bosom of a parent, reposing in the sense of security, assured by hearing and feeling the "heartbeat of God." I suspect that anyone who claims to have permanently "arrived" in the "unseen" perspective is bogus, and filled with spiritual pride. Conversely, when we begin to taste and see God's perspective, one is all the more aware of their own frailty and foibles and failures, convinced and convicted of sin that misrepresents who we are in Christ. God will no doubt take me farther into His presence and workings, but I am quite satisfied to this point with what I have seen of God and His ways. What is your heart's desire?

All I have attempted to do is give you a glimpse of what I have periodically seen by the revelation of God, the possibility of the "unseen" perspective as we participate and express the character of God in the midst of the experiences of life; and if God speaks to your heart in the process, then praise God! To God be the glory! It is an "unseen" perspective that I have found very satisfying in my own life.

In the Christmas song, *The Little Drummer Boy*, we find these words: "Said the night wind to the little lamb, *do you see what I see...?* Said the little lamb to the shepherd boy, *do you hear what I hear...?*" These questions are asked in reference to the advent of Jesus. The same question can be continuously asked by Christians as the awareness of Christ's sufficient grace-function operates in their lives: "Do you see what I see? Do you hear what I hear?"

I can only hope this comprehensive diagram of the House of Christian Contrasts that we are using in this study allows you to get a glimpse of what I have begun to see (at least as a possibility), and what I have faintly heard as "the still small voice of God." Please realize that this diagram is just another organizing structure by which we can put together some of what might have appeared to be disparate truths of Christian thought. It has been a meaningful and exciting tool for me, a mental picture with which to organize my thoughts, and draw me into a deeper spirituality. If the diagram works for you and helps you to see a more comprehensive structure for Christian thought, so be it! If not, God is faithful to give you a personal "revelation" for understanding and experiencing His gospel, His "good news," which is nothing more (and nothing less) than **JESUS**.

By means of the spiritually operative *"diaffective* process," we can begin to "move through" the self-evaluative "affects" of the "seen" context of our lives here on earth, and participate experientially in the "unseen" realities of God's divine and mysterious working in our lives. This necessitates that we be receptive to such by our response of faith ("our receptivity of His activity"), trusting that God is at work even when we cannot see or understand what He is doing.

This continuous movement from the "seen" to the "unseen" is a counter-intuitive perspective of what is transpiring in our human lives. Only those in whom Christ lives and reigns will have the capability of participating and understanding this other-worldly process. Only the Christ-one, the Christian, who is responding in faith to what God is doing will experience "the eternal weight of glory" as God presses us into conformity with, and visible expression of His glorious character.

The remainder of this volume is a sequence of diagrams of the top-tier, the pinnacle, of what we have considered in the "House of Christian Contrasts." These diagrams attempt to give some examples of how we often react to the experiences of life from a natural, visible "seen" perspective, and allow our self-oriented reaction to "affect" how we see ourselves, others, the world, and God Himself. The diagrams are to be read from the bottom to the top (yes, even that is counterintuitive).

As one reads these diagrams from the bottom up, the reader will recognize and personalize some of the inevitable "experiences" of life, and our natural human reactions to what we see going on around us and in us. The Christian will recognize that he has a supernatural provision in the Spirit of Christ dwelling within to "move through" (*diaffective*) the natural affects and reactions in the "seen" perspective in order to respond with faith to whatever God has in mind in our lives in the "unseen" perspective.

Some will find these diagrammatic contrasts of the movement from the "seen" to the "unseen" to be helpful. Others may find them simply confusing. To understand the diagrams or even the entire thesis of contrasts in this book is not the real objective. The objective is that every Christ-indwelt Christian might recognize that they are "created for His glory" (Isa. 43:7), and participate in the grace-dynamic of God's activity as they respond by faith. We want to be "in on" what God is "up to" – participating with God.

Eternal Weight of Glory

UNSEEN

Supernatural perceptual level - eternal, the divine realm of the Spirit, invisible, interiority. God is at work! The realm of "mystery."

SEEN

Natural perceptual level - temporal, time-based, visible, visceral, empirical, level of the senses. What is going on here? Must get it analyzed.

Experiences

Eternal Weight of Glory

UNSEEN

Hang on for the ride; go with the flow of God's grace. Can't get it all figured out; unknown factor. WWJD - Watching what Jesus does?

SEEN

We attempt to control and manipulate the situation. Get it figured out; get a handle on it. WWJD - What would Jesus do?

Experiences

Eternal Weight of Glory

UNSEEN

Doing is not as important as being. Knowing who we are "in Christ;" being available to His action. Awareness and appreciation for what God is doing.

SEEN

See the problem, then do something about it. Just do it! (Nike). Jesus is helper; a come-along. Me and Jesus, we can do it! Produce for God.

Experiences

Eternal Weight of Glory

UNSEEN

Process and people more important than progress. God-oriented, rather than goal-oriented. Emphasis on what God has done, and is doing.

SEEN

Progress is important in "seen" world. Must set your goals and strive to achieve. Life is an upward climb. "Pressing on the upward way."

Experiences

Eternal Weight of Glory

UNSEEN

FAITH is beyond correct calculations of content.
Faith is the dynamic "receptivity of His activity."
Faith allows us to soar on "wings like eagles."

SEEN

One's philosophy and belief is the key to success.
Christianity is a belief-system; correct perception.
Grounded in the "word;" here I stand (epistemology)

Experiences

Eternal Weight of Glory

UNSEEN

Potholes of life are an irrelevancy. They become "speed bumps" in our lives, to get our attention.
Focus in on the opportunities, not the obstacles.

SEEN

Potholes of life become big issue - focus of life.
Tend to live in the "pothole avoidance mode;"
Avoidance of immorality and heresy.

Experiences

Eternal Weight of Glory

UNSEEN

Situations of life viewed as opportunities that are "thrown in front of us" to show that we "have what it takes in Christ Jesus." ...Trajectory.

SEEN

Hardships of life viewed as roadblocks, obstacles, hurdles that we must jump over. Tragedy of falling. Problem: pro=before; ballo=to throw. God? Satan?

| Experiences |

- -

Eternal Weight of Glory

UNSEEN

Stuff happens! Life is messy! With 20/20 hindsight of faith, we usually look back and say, "That's the best thing that could have happened."

SEEN

Life is hard! The trials of life can overwhelm and bury a person under the pile. Makes us give-up. "Does God like to see people suffer?"

| Experiences |

Eternal Weight of Glory

UNSEEN

"All things work for good..." (Rom. 8:28)
This thing did not surprise God. God is panic-proof.
We begin to "see God in everything...circumstance"

SEEN

"This is terrible ... a catastrophe; the worst thing that could happen to me." "Where is God when you need Him? Why would God allow this?"

Experiences

Eternal Weight of Glory

UNSEEN

Relational awareness of God's love. When we know without a shadow of a doubt that God loves us. "I am accepted in the Beloved" (Eph. 1:6)

SEEN

How can you say "God is love" when He allows all this suffering in life?" Either God is not love, or He is not all-powerful to cause evil to cease

Experiences

Eternal Weight of Glory

UNSEEN

Seeing through God's eyes ... spiritual perspective
"I wouldn't have seen it, if I hadn't believed it."
Song - "Turn your eyes upon Jesus ..."

SEEN

Present situation looms large in our vision.
"I wouldn't have believed it, if I hadn't see it!"
Reality is what eyes see, and mind perceives.

Experiences

Eternal Weight of Glory

UNSEEN

As a Christ-one, I have the "mind of Christ."
I can begin to see that what happens in the world
should serve as springboards for character of Christ.

SEEN

What happens in the world around me affects me!
Makes me feel inadequate, fearful, defensive, likely
to respond with fight, fright, flight. "I'm only human!"

Experiences

Eternal Weight of Glory

UNSEEN

God speaks to us in a "still small voice" (I Kgs 19:12) With the Spirit of Christ within our spirit, we have an inner prompting that leads us.

SEEN

World barrages us with clamoring voices, telling us what we should desire, need, and want.
With loud volume advertising screams at us.

Experiences

Eternal Weight of Glory

UNSEEN

God's ways are "past finding out," & "fresh every morning." God is spontaneous, unpredictable, unique, novel, and treats us as individuals.

SEEN

Procedural techniques the world advocates are so predictable and monotonous – rules & regulations.
Like manna, "the same every day"

Experiences

Eternal Weight of Glory

UNSEEN

Man is a dependent, derivative creature of God. Our identity, nature, character, and destiny are derived from a spiritual source.

SEEN

"You have what it takes." "You can do it." "Give it your best effort." "Be all you can be." "Derivativeness is tyranny" - someone controlling you.

Experiences

Eternal Weight of Glory

UNSEEN

C.S. Lewis - "Pain is God's megaphone to rouse a deaf world." In a fallen world, pain is inevitable, but misery is optional.

SEEN

Pain-avoidance is major concern of "seen" world. "Deliver me." "Heal me." Flock to hospitals, clinics, doctors, medicines, sedatives, pain-killers.

Experiences

Eternal Weight of Glory

UNSEEN

God rejoices when we come to the "end of ourself;" when we are willing to DIE to all our self-efforts, and allow living Lord Jesus Christ to be our life.

SEEN

Fear of death is universal in fallen world.
Yet, the frustration of trials and reactions to trials leads some to say, "I would rather die, than continue."

Experiences

Eternal Weight of Glory

UNSEEN

God's objective is that we experience His JOY. Greek word is <u>chara</u>, requiring <u>charis</u> (grace) in Jesus Christ. Not based on chance circumstances.

SEEN

"Right to pursue happiness." <u>hap</u>=chance.
As happenstances happen haphazardly, one might happen to be happy, perhaps if no mishaps.

Experiences

Eternal Weight of Glory

UNSEEN

"Unseen" perspective often called "Idealism"
Cannot empirically verify. "God is Spirit, and we worship Him in spirit and in truth" (Jn 4:24).

SEEN

"Seen" perspective and reactions called "Realism"
The physical and the psychological are the "real world." Our hope is in human potential.

Experiences

Eternal Weight of Glory

UNSEEN

Greek word for thanksgiving is <u>eucharist</u>– <u>eu</u>=good; <u>charis</u>=grace. Giving thanks is recognizing the "good grace" of God for all things...in all things.

SEEN

Society tells us that we should be thankful.
We need more of the "gratitude attitude."
Special day set aside as "Thanksgiving Day."

Experiences

Eternal Weight of Glory

UNSEEN

"Knowing" of personal intimacy with God most important. Wisdom = seeing from God's perspective. "That I may know Him, & power of His resurrection"

SEEN

World places premium on intellectual knowledge. Education, degrees, credentials regarded important. Wisdom = best application of knowledge.

Experiences

Eternal Weight of Glory

UNSEEN

Satan is the "god of this world." World cannot be saved! World is going to do what the world is going to do. "The battle is the Lord's" (I Sam. 17:47)

SEEN

"The world is going to hell in a hand-basket!" We need to solve the world's problems, change the culture, save the world, build "Christian nation."

Experiences

Eternal Weight of Glory

UNSEEN

Take time to ponder, pray, "listen to God" to determine what He wants to be and do in situation. Then we respond in faith-receptivity of His activity.

SEEN

Human reactions to situations. Immediate, split-second reaction time, in accord with our "flesh" patterns of self-defense.

Experiences

- -

Eternal Weight of Glory

UNSEEN

God's ways have no linear cause and effect. Why? Just because God directed us in this way. Usefulness of uselessness; uselessness of usefulness.

SEEN

World wants all our decisions to serve logical, useful purpose for betterment of mankind. Efficiency, practicality, pragmatism, productivity.

Experiences

Eternal Weight of Glory

UNSEEN

The circumstances of living here on earth are not eternal. Many problems are just pesky irrelevancies. Here today, gone tomorrow. ... NPG -"body-fuss"

SEEN

Our reactions to situations often don't make sense. There is a sense of irony & futility, even anxiety & dread that our choices aren't going to solve things.

Experiences

Eternal Weight of Glory

UNSEEN

No one promised that life would be equitable or fair. We are only responsible for choice of response. We have faith in the faithfulness & justice of God.

SEEN

Annoyance and irritation at how unfair life is. Life sucks! "Makes me furious, outraged, angry." Satan's "fight" reaction.

Experiences

Eternal Weight of Glory

UNSEEN

None of us are adequate in ourselves (II Cor. 3:5) "I can do all things thru Christ who strengthens me. (Phil. 4:13) "Perfect love casts our fear" (I Jn 4:18)

SEEN

Stress of life makes me worry that I can't handle the circumstances of life. Consternation, anxiety, paranoia, worry. Satan's "fright" reaction.

Experiences

Eternal Weight of Glory

UNSEEN

Christ is our reason for living. "Christ Jesus is our HOPE" (I Tim. 1:1). "Christ in us, the hope of glory" (Col. 1:27). Expectation of far better in Him.

SEEN

"The pain is too much. I can't take it anymore. It's not worth living. Desperation, hopelessness, SUICIDE Satan's ultimate "flight" reaction.

Experiences

Eternal Weight of Glory

UNSEEN

It's all about HIM! Our place should be that of lowliness and humility. John the Baptist's response: "I must decrease; He must increase" (Jn. 3:30)

SEEN

Epidemic of narcissism in our society.
"It's all about ME; what I like, what I want."
Satan's character of selfish preoccupation.

Experiences

Eternal Weight of Glory

UNSEEN

"In as much as we do it to the least of these, we do it unto Him" (Matt. 25:40). We accept every person as the intended container of Christ's presence.

SEEN

In our self-concern and elevated perspective of ourself, others are pushed aside in REJECTION. Regrettable that others get run over in process.

Experiences

Eternal Weight of Glory

UNSEEN

We can experience rest and tranquility in the presence of God. "I am only responsible to be and to do, what God wants to be and do in me today."

SEEN

Exhausted with the hustle & bustle of hectic schedules. Never-ending bombardment of things people want us to do. Life in the fast lane!

Experiences

Eternal Weight of Glory

UNSEEN

"Set your minds on things above" (Col. 3:2)
"Whatever is true, honorable, right, purse, lovely, of good repute ... think on these things" (Phil. 4:8)

SEEN

Preoccupied with mental thought-processes. Attempt to determine correct thinking – "political correctness," or "orthodox doctrine."

Experiences

Eternal Weight of Glory

UNSEEN

Fellowship requires genuine, transparent investment in other's lives. We need each other, in order to be the "people of God."

SEEN

Conversation & communication is reduced to digital e-mails and text messages. People isolate themselves and prefer anonymity of electronic devices.

Experiences

Eternal Weight of Glory

UNSEEN

Qualitative analysis of success. Character of Christ is the objective. "Fruit of the Spirit is love, joy, peace, patience, kindness, goodness, ... (Gal. 5:22,23)

SEEN

Quantitative analysis of success. Bigger is better! Church is evaluated by numbers and statistics. Three big Bs: buildings, budgets, baptisms

Experiences

Eternal Weight of Glory

UNSEEN

Church encourages deeper relationship with God.
"Be still, and know that I am God" (Ps. 46:10)
"He who has ears to hear, let him hear." (Rom. 8)

SEEN

Religion advocates action: go, go, go; do, do, do!
Encourage involvement: "Mary had a little lamb,..."
Emphasis on authority, involvement, performance...

Experiences

Eternal Weight of Glory

UNSEEN

Church is meant to be the intimate relational interaction of those in whom Christ lives and loves. Real, genuine, relational transparency.

SEEN

Religion is talk, talk, talk; teach, teach, teach.
Incessant conversations about correct doctrine.
The believe-right religion is deafening.

Experiences

Eternal Weight of Glory

UNSEEN

Security is in the intimacy of one's relationship with the living Christ. "Spirit bears witness with my spirit that I am a child of God" (Rom. 8:16)

SEEN

Religion is concerned about security. Have we done right things to be assured of eternal salvation? Walked the aisle, repeated statement of faith.

Experiences

Eternal Weight of Glory

UNSEEN

Prayer is the breath of one's life. "Pray without ceasing" (I Thess. 5:17). "Yes, Lord .. You are all I need, my sufficiency in this situation."

SEEN

Religion views prayer as an escape hatch. Ask God to deliver from problems, for strength in problems. Imperative importance of saying our prayers.

Experiences

Eternal Weight of Glory

UNSEEN

Christian giving is Divine Giver dwelling in Christian, advising what we're to give, to whom we should give, where and by what means.

SEEN

Religion has insatiable thirst for finances.
Emphasize 10% tithing as God's commanded mandate.
Assessment to finance the institution.

Experiences

Eternal Weight of Glory

UNSEEN

The Will of God is always and only JESUS. God desires to see the character of Jesus lived out in the behavior of His people.

SEEN

Religion attempts to figure out the specific "will of God." Will of God seen like a maze, full of dead-ends, and wrong turns.

Experiences

Eternal Weight of Glory

UNSEEN

Christianity views "obedience" in relational paradigm. Obedience is to "listen under" (hupakouo) the voice of God in personal hearing of His direction.

SEEN

Religion views "obedience" in legal paradigm. To obey God is to keep the rules and regulations, the "thou shalt" & "thou shalt nots" of the Law.

Experiences

- -

Eternal Weight of Glory

UNSEEN

Repentance (metanoia) - change of mind leading to change of action. Change of mind=I can't, but He can. Change of action=by faith I will let God act.

SEEN

Religious perspective of "repentance" is remorse for wrong actions or wrong, erroneous thinking. Must turn over a new leaf, and assent to truth.

Experiences

Eternal Weight of Glory

UNSEEN

Salvation is an integral union with living Savior. Salvation is the process whereby the Savior "makes us safe" from self-destructive self-effort.

SEEN

Religion views salvation as a commodity that we can make our possession. Someone "gets saved," and thus has salvation in pocket as passport to heaven.

Experiences

Eternal Weight of Glory

UNSEEN

Christian social action is to love people in our community, expressing the character of Christ relationally to all we interact with.

SEEN

Religion focuses on need to "change the culture." Social action in campaigns against immorality and pornography using petitions and boycotts.

Experiences

Eternal Weight of Glory

UNSEEN

Church of Christ meant to function by spiritual giftedness of every Christian "led of the Spirit" to allow Christ to minister to others through them.

SEEN

Religion – church should function like business with hierarchical structure, flow of command and authority of pastors, elders, and shepherds.

Experiences

Eternal Weight of Glory

UNSEEN

Joshua and Caleb saw same things, but seeing the unseen power of God, they reported, "Let us go. God has given us the land. We will overcome!"

SEEN

Twelve spies from Israel went into Canaan for reconnaissance. Ten came back: "Giants in the land." "We were as grasshoppers." "We will be slaughtered."

Experiences

Eternal Weight of Glory

UNSEEN

"Image of God" is functional visible expression of the invisible character of God in human behavior, allowing us to fulfill purpose of our creation.

SEEN

Religion views the "image of God" as something about human beings that is "like God," a natural representation or reflection of God in man.

Experiences

Eternal Weight of Glory

UNSEEN

With eternal perspective, we can respond by allowing the divine Forgiver within us to respond, "Father, forgive them; they know not what they do."

SEEN

With temporal perspective, we may react with vengeance, seeking to retaliate against the one we think has wronged us.

Experiences

Eternal Weight of Glory

UNSEEN

Willing to "stand-under" the Lordship of the living Lord Jesus, despite our inability to understand what is happening in the situation.

SEEN

We calculate with human reasoning in order to understand the situation, and figure out our next course of action.

Experiences

Eternal Weight of Glory

UNSEEN

We rely on expectations of "hope" that the Lord Jesus will control and act in the situation in a manner that brings glory to Himself.

SEEN

We have projected expectations of our human potential and ability to remedy a situation with well-organized self-effort.

Experiences

Eternal Weight of Glory

UNSEEN

In the receptivity of faith, we are desirous that God in Christ might do as He wills in the midst of the situation that confronts us.

SEEN

We resolve to act in self-sufficiency to solve the problem that confronts us, seeking to make the situation better (i.e. to our liking).

Experiences

Eternal Weight of Glory

UNSEEN

The Christian individual can respond by allowing God's Grace to function, allowing Jesus Christ to DO what He desires in the midst of the situation.

SEEN

Humans have a natural propensity to spring into action to DO what is considered necessary to resolve their perceived problems with self-effort.

Experiences

CONCLUSION

Let us review the development of what we have called the "House of Christian Contrasts"

We began with the Foundation of the *Either/ors* which exist in a Diametric Polarity with each other.

We noted the "ultimate incongruity" of how an angelic derivative creature like Lucifer could possibly have made what appears to have been an underived choice to defy God and manifest selfish character contrary to God's character, thereby becoming the antagonist of God, the fixed negative of God's positive, the adversary, the devil, the Evil One, Satan.

The next mind-blower was how a diametric polarity could possibly become a dialectic reciprocity, how an either/or like the "wholly other" qualitative difference between God and man, could be transformed into a both/and God-man in the person of Jesus Christ.

That required the *Absolute Paradox*, as Kierkegaard suggested, the incarnational conundrum of the Son of God being born in a manger in Bethlehem, which to this very day we celebrate at Christmas.

The Dialectic Reciprocity of allowing ideas and concepts to exist in indefinite tension in the both/and framework of our Christian thinking is very difficult, especially for Western thinkers steeped in the "one or the other" thinking of Aristotle. Accepting the *Both/ands* of ideas that constantly talk back and forth with one another without trying to nail down one or the other is a skill that many Christian thinkers have a difficult time juggling in their minds.

But then, the transition between the both/ands and the "seen/unseen" level of the experiential is also a miraculous and supernatural occurrence. Unless the risen and living Lord Jesus is brought to life in our spirit by a "new birth," then all we have is theoretical ideology or Christian philosophy and theology. The spiritual reality of the Christ-life must come into dynamic reality within us via the *"Unfathomable Inclusion"* of our participation in the very life of Jesus Christ.

Only then can we experience the *"Diaffective Process"* whereby we "move through" the natural human "affects" of life that cause us to react with self-concern and self-interest, and venture into the counterintuitive perspective of the spiritual "unseen" whereby we allow the Triune God to LOVE "others" as the primary focus of our lives.

And all of this process of God's functioning in our lives is intended to exhibit the eternal GLORY of God.

Notice again that the entire process of this structure of contrasts that we have been illustrating is beyond the natural abilities of humanity – beyond human ability to understand and explain, as well as beyond human ability to implement and orchestrate. In particular, we might note the improbable transitions from one part of the structure to the next, evidencing the inconceivability of all that God has done and is doing in Jesus Christ.

Initially we start with the "**Ultimate Incongruity**" of how evil could enter into the good and righteous creation of god, allowing Satan's solicitations to provide the genuine alternative spiritual choice that humanity could/would confront.

Then we come to the "**Absolute Paradox**" of how an antithetical either/or of the Creator-God and the creature-man could become a both/and God-man in the Person of Jesus Christ, allowing for the "one Mediator between God and man to reconcile the faith-love relationship between God and human beings.

We add to that the **"Indefinite Tension"** of the necessary balance of the both/and categories of doctrinal ideas, befuddling our natural desire for absolute certainty wherein we think we can figure out God and His ways and control the truth of God.

Then comes the "**Unfathomable Inclusion**" wherein every receptive human individual can go beyond mere assent to the theological and doctrinal tenets, and can enter into participation in the very life of the risen and living Lord Jesus, to experience and re-present His life as we become part of the gospel narrative.

Within that spiritual union with Jesus Christ, we can experience the "**Counter-intuitive Perception**" of seeing the "unseen" presence and activity of God at work in all things, and specifically in our own lives.

And we are drawn into an ever-closer relational oneness with God as He embraces us and draws us into Himself with an unchangeable "**Eternal Weight of**

Glory" wherein He is glorified, and our purpose for being is fulfilled, having been "created for His glory" (Isa. 43:70.

Do we realize how amazing it is to be included and involved in God's plan via His Son, Jesus Christ, and by the power of the Holy Spirit? It is more glorious that any of us can ask or think, or even begin to put into words and explanation. We are *in on* what God is *up to*! That is the "good news" of the gospel, explaining how man's intended relationship with the God of the universe fell apart in sin, but is restored in Jesus Christ to an unimaginable participation of loving, relational union and intimacy with the Triune God, in the "holy place" of His heavenly presence.

But it should also cause us to remember that such a construction as we have been looking at will indeed seem outlandish to the "natural man" without spiritual understanding. It is no wonder that we cannot expect to reason an individual to faith in Jesus Christ via an "ultimate incongruity," "absolute paradox," "indefinite tension," "unfathomable inclusion," "counter-intuitive perception," and an "inexplicable weight of glory."

Perhaps you have thought (as I once did) that any reasonable person would become a "Christian" if we could just articulate the gospel in a logical explanation. The Christian gospel cannot be explained by natural logical reason alone. That is not to say that it is not a reasonable faith that we have, but only that GOD alone can bring enlightenment and illumination to the minds that have been blinded by Satan (II Cor. 4:4). The revelation of God must strike fire in a person's heart, and then we can see the Theo-logic, the God-logic, in all that

God has done and is doing. It will always be inconceivable to natural human logic.

I am thoroughly convinced that it is extremely important for Christian people to see the perspective of this Christian House of Contrasts, in order to see what God has done and is doing among His people.

The mental construct of "The House of Christian Contrasts" presented in this book may appear to some to be rather theoretical; a conjectural and hypothetical abstraction of how Christian thought might be formulated. In the language of those engaged in physical and material home construction, it might be thought of as a "spec house," a structure built with the speculative hope that someone should come along and buy it as their place to live.

This admittedly conjectural construct of thought is an attempt to view the integrity and consistency of Christian thought, to see how one element builds upon another to form the total structure, from the foundation to the pinnacle, from bottom to top. And all of it must be built on the "rock" of God's revelation through His Son, Jesus Christ.

When Jesus was charged with drawing from a spiritual source contrary to His own being, from Satan rather than God, He explained that such an incongruity is not logically feasible: "If a house is divided against itself, that house will not be able to stand" (Matt. 12:25; Mk. 3:25; Lk. 11:17), was His reply. There must be organizational integrity in the construction of a building, as well as in the construction of our thinking. This study has been an attempt to provide a perspective of such integral consistency in Christian thought.

It is the author's desire that this blueprinting of Christian thought might provide a meaningful formatting to view the integrity of Christian thought in the minds of thinking Christians. Beyond that, it is the author's desire that this construct of thought might be translated into an individual Christian's spiritual and experiential expression of the life and character of the risen Lord Jesus in the embodiment of their particular physical "house" (cf. II Cor. 5:1,2), i.e. in their physical existence as a Christian in this world. Beyond the individual Christian expression, we must also recognize the "house" of our collective Christian expression in the church, in the collective gathering of those in whom Christ lives, designated as "the house/household of God" (Eph. 2:19; I Tim. 3:15; Heb. 3:6; 10:21; I Pet. 2:5). The collective community of the *ecclesia*-assembly of God's people "in Christ" evidences the cooperative stability of Christians standing together in the "household of God."

We must ever remember that it is the Divine Builder who constructs "the house of Christian contrasts." "The builder of the house is God" (Heb. 3:3,4). If God doesn't build the house it is not worth building, and will eventually collapse under its own weight, never manifesting "the eternal weight of glory" (II Cor. 4:17) whereby the Triune God is radiated, expressed, and made known.

Additional books authored by Jim Fowler available on Amazon.com

Man as God Intended
Christ at Work in You
Christianity is NOT Religion
Christmas: It's History and Meaning
The Divine Drama of Love
The Extent and Efficacy of the Life and Work of Jesus Christ
A Commentary on the Four Gospels
A Commentary on the Epistle to the Galatians
A Commentary on the Epistle to the Hebrews
A Commentary on the Revelation of John
In the Beginning, God Created
Ninety-five Theses for the Twenty-first Century Church
Spirit-union Allows for Soul-rest
The Triune God in Christian Thought and Experience
Union with Christ
What's That in Your Hand?
Parodies of Piety: Everything I Never Learned in Sunday School
Frequently Asked Questions
Chicken Bones of Christian Thought
Two Sides of Every Coin: A Dialectic Formatting of Christian Thought
Derivative Man
A Synopsis and Personal Appraisal of the Theology of Thomas F. Torrance
The Issue is JESUS: Daily Thoughts for Thoughtful Christians
Pneumatikois: Spiritual Things

All of these books can be viewed at:
https://www.amazon.com/-/e/B00LWU9CHE

www.ingramcontent.com/pod-product-compliance
Lightning Source LLC
Chambersburg PA
CBHW070640050426
42451CB00008B/233